An Evaluation of Existing Vegetation Data and Data Gaps Leading to Inventories and Forest Management Recommendations at Mount Joy and Mount Misery at Valley Forge National Historical Park

Natural Resource Technical Report NPS/NER/NRTR—2013/670

Marc D. Abrams and Sarah E. Johnson

307 Forest Resources Building
School of Forest Resources
Penn State University
University Park, PA 16802 USA

January 2013

U.S. Department of the Interior
National Park Service
Natural Resource Stewardship and Science
Fort Collins, Colorado

The National Park Service, Natural Resource Stewardship and Science office in Fort Collins, Colorado, publishes a range of reports that address natural resource topics. These reports are of interest and applicability to a broad audience in the National Park Service and others in natural resource management, including scientists, conservation and environmental constituencies, and the public.

The Natural Resource Technical Report Series is used to disseminate results of scientific studies in the physical, biological, and social sciences for both the advancement of science and the achievement of the National Park Service mission. The series provides contributors with a forum for displaying comprehensive data that are often deleted from journals because of page limitations.

All manuscripts in the series receive the appropriate level of peer review to ensure that the information is scientifically credible, technically accurate, appropriately written for the intended audience, and designed and published in a professional manner. This report received informal peer review by subject-matter experts who were not directly involved in the collection, analysis, or reporting of the data.

Views, statements, findings, conclusions, recommendations, and data in this report do not necessarily reflect views and policies of the National Park Service, U.S. Department of the Interior. Mention of trade names or commercial products does not constitute endorsement or recommendation for use by the U.S. Government.

This report is available from the Natural Resource Publications Management website (http://www.nature.nps.gov/publications/nrpm/).

Please cite this publication as:

Abrams, M. D., and S. E. Johnson. 2013. An evaluation of existing vegetation data and data gaps leading to inventories and forest management recommendations at Mount Joy and Mount Misery at Valley Forge National Historical Park. Natural Resource Technical Report NPS/NER/NRTR—2013/670. National Park Service, Fort Collins, Colorado.

NPS 464/119618, January 2013

Contents

Contents (Continued)

Figures

Figures (Continued)

Tables

Tables (Continued)

Tables (Continued)

Tables (Continued)

Appendixes

Executive Summary

A fixed-plot, long-term monitoring system was implemented in 1992 to evaluate vegetative communities in two large wooded areas at Valley Forge National Historical Park (NHP). This included 30 paired 2×2-m fenced and unfenced vegetation plots (15 in each area of Mount Joy and Mount Misery). These plots were resurveyed in 1993, 1995–96, 1998, 2003, and 2010. In addition, collection and analyses were conducted of new overstory and understory vegetation data in 20×20-m permanently marked plots in 2010 in the Dry Oak Forest stand on Mount Misery and the Dry Oak Forest stand and Successional Tuliptree Forest stand on Mount Joy. Twenty plots per stand were co-located (when appropriate and possible to do so) with the unfenced long-term vegetation monitoring plots on Mount Misery and Mount Joy. The objectives of this collective monitoring system are to: 1) describe the existing overstory and understory plant community on Mount Misery and Mount Joy in terms of species richness and abundance; and 2) determine changes in abundance and species composition of understory plant communities in fenced and unfenced plots over time. This report includes: (1) the monitoring protocol and timing for future data collection; (2) understory vegetation trends over time (1992–2010) for the 30 paired 2×2-m fenced and unfenced plots; (3) understory and overstory vegetation data from the sixty 20×20-m plots; (4) management prescriptions to close the gap between existing and desired forest conditions (primarily mixed-oak/hickory based on Largay and Sneddon [2007]); (5) minimum management prescriptions considered necessary (assuming white-tailed deer [*Odocoileus virginianus*] densities of 31–35 deer per forested sq mi) to promote tree regeneration regardless of species composition; and (6) successional trajectory in the absence of active forest management.

Twenty-one species of trees were recorded in the 20×20-m overstory plots in the Successional Tuliptree Forest on Mount Joy, dominated by tuliptree (*Liriodendron tulipifera*; 50% relative importance value), followed by red maple (*Acer rubrum*; 7%) and white ash (*Fraxinus americana*; 6%). Five oak species (*Quercus* spp) were recorded on the site, with relative importance values ranging from 1–3%. Japanese stiltgrass (*Microstegium vimineum*) dominated (72% cover) the forest understory. Twenty-one tree species were recorded in the Dry Oak Forest on Mount Joy, including scarlet oak (*Q. coccinea*), black oak (*Q. velutina*), chestnut oak (*Q. prinus* or Q. *montana*), red oak (*Q. rubra*), and white oak (*Q. alba*), with a combined 40% relative importance value. Fourteen tree species were recorded in the Dry Oak Forest on Mount Misery, including five oak species with a combined 51% relative importance value. Sapling and seedling densities were low to moderate (500 and 10,000 stems per ha, respectively) in each of the three stands and were primarily shade-tolerant red maple, blackgum (*Nyssa sylvatica*), and sassafras (*Sassafras albidum*). Numbers of oak seedlings and saplings were particularly low to nonexistent in all three stands, with the exception of chestnut oak seedlings (875 per ha) on Mount Misery. Similarly, the unfenced 2×2-m plots in all three stands had low densities of seedlings and saplings, especially concerning oak. In contrast, the fenced plots contained an overall average of 33,133 seedlings per ha and were dominated by chestnut oak, followed by red maple, sassafras, blackgum, and white ash; however, the Successional Tuliptree Forest on Mount Joy contained lower overall seedling and oak seedling densities than the Dry Oak Forest stands. Very few saplings of any species of tree were recorded in the 18-year-old fenced plots, and none of them were oak.

Species richness in both the fenced and unfenced plots was greater on Mount Joy than on Mount Misery. In both areas, richness generally increased over time in fenced plots, but exhibited a slight decline over time in unfenced plots. The number of exotic species in the fenced and unfenced plots on Mount Misery was low, but was highest in 1993 (mostly in fenced plots) and then declined through 2010. On Mount Joy, the number of exotic species in both fenced and unfenced plots was much higher than on Mount Misery for all survey years, with peak numbers in 2003. This was due to a large increase in exotics in the fenced plots during that year. In 2003, five herbaceous species present at Valley Forge NHP were proposed as potential indicator species of the effects of deer browsing. In 2010, these species occurred in six of 30 fenced plots (1–3 species/stand), and one species (Jack-in-the-pulpit; *Arisaema triphyllum*) was present in four of 30 unfenced plots. The deer browse indicator species occurred more frequently on Mount Joy than Mount Misery. We conclude that regeneration stocking of tree species that are desirable according to Largay and Sneddon (2007; mainly oak) was inadequate even in the fenced plots because of the low height of the existing seedlings; however, 50% of the fenced plots were adequately stocked when all tree species (including those considered non-desirable by Largay and Sneddon, 2007) are considered. Forest management recommendations are proposed to foster increased target species regeneration and recruitment across the oak and tuliptree forests, including the harvesting of non-target trees, herbicide application to cut stumps and Japanese stiltgrass, and planting seedlings of targeted tree species.

Acknowledgments

We thank Mr. Ben Sands for assistance with data collection in the spring of 2010 and the summary and analysis of those data.

Introduction

Long-term studies of forest dynamics indicate that oak (*Quercus*) species dominated much of the eastern U.S. forest biome during the last 5,000–7,000 years (reviewed in Abrams 2002, Abrams and Nowacki 2008). Oak dominance was fairly constant during the millennia and was associated with periodic fire (Abrams 1992, 2002, Delcourt and Delcourt 1997, Lorimer and White 2003). Native American populations increased throughout eastern North America during the Holocene and so did their use of fire, land clearing, and other silvicultural activities (Whitney 1994, Abrams and Nowacki 2008, Nowacki and Abrams 2008). Thus, low to moderate levels of biotic and abiotic disturbance and climate change were an intrinsic part of the Holocene ecology; resulting in a dynamic equilibrium in oak forest structure and composition. Most authors believe that fire played an important role in the historical development and perpetuation of eastern oak forests prior to European settlement (Lorimer 1985, Abrams 1992, Ducey et al. 1996).

Following European settlement, the magnitude of anthropogenic disturbances in eastern U.S. forests changed dramatically. This included extensive clearcutting, often followed by catastrophic fire, then the onset of the fire control era in the early 20th century (Smokey the Bear era), and the introduction of exotic insects and diseases (Abrams 1998, Nowacki and Abrams 2008). All of these have led to unprecedented and rapid changes in forest composition (Schuster et al. 2008). This is particularly true for the eastern United States that has seen the extirpation of the once dominant American chestnut (*Castanea dentata*) overstory from blight, loss of vast areas of white pine (*Pinus strobus*) forests from logging followed by intense fires, a virtual cessation of oak recruitment from fire suppression and intensive deer browsing, and a rapid increase in native and exotic invasives (Abrams 1992, Whitney 1994, Abrams 1998).

One of the most dramatic changes that occurred in forests of eastern North America during the 20th century was the increase in red maple (*Acer rubrum*) (Kittredge and Ashton 1990, Abrams 1998, Fei and Steiner 2007, 2009, Schuster et al. 2008). The increase in red maple is thought to be related, at least in part, to the exclusion of fire in most oak forests, as well as its ability to increase following logging events (Lorimer 1985, Abrams 1992, Abrams and Nowacki 1992, Fei and Steiner 2009). Presently, red maple dominates the understory and mid-canopy of many eastern oak forests, and it appears, to the detriment of oak, that it will increase in the overstory during the next century (Abrams 1998). The increase in red maple and other shade-tolerant, non-pyrogenic species has contributed to the "mesophication" process in many eastern oak forests, reducing the likelihood of restoring the natural fire cycle in these forests (Nowacki and Abrams 2008). It is thought that low-to-moderate understory fire and moderate-to-large canopy openings (i.e., not single tree gaps) are needed for the long-term sustainability of most eastern oak forests (Lorimer 1985, Kittredge and Ashton 1990, Abrams 1992, 2003). In some areas, however, the lack of fire has allowed volatile live fuels, such as mountain-laurel (*Kalmia latifolia*) and other ericaceous species, to increase in density and stature, predisposing many oak-hickory forests to intense fires that would not be representative of the historical low-intensity fire regime (McGee et al. 1995, Moser et al. 1996, Nowacki and Abrams 2008).

Given current conditions of the ecology and management of eastern oak forests, the increasing overstory importance of red maple and other later-successional, shade-tolerant species, such as beech (*Fagus grandifolia*), sugar maple (*Acer saccharum*), and blackgum (*Nyssa sylvatica*), seems inevitable. This may be most apparent on mesic or dry-mesic sites rather than on xeric sites, where the oak replacement species are less aggressive (Abrams 1992, Schuster et al. 2008). The loss of oak domination in eastern U. S. forests will be one of the primary consequences of the continued expansion of later successional tree species on sub-xeric sites. This research investigated the overstory and understory composition for oak and tuliptree forests in Valley Forge National Historical Park, Pennsylvania.

The dominants of dry oak forests, chestnut oak (*Q. prinus or montana*), scarlet oak (*Q. coccinea*), and black oak (*Q. velutina*), are light-demanding species that are also favored browse species (both foliage and acorns) of deer and small mammals. Unmanaged oak forests with high white-tailed deer (*Odocoileus virginianus*) densities are not regenerating oak (and other favored tree species) due to the impact of high shade in the understory and deer browsing. These forests will change during the forest succession process to less favored trees species such as red maple, blackgum, birch (*Betula* spp.), black cherry (*Prunus serotina*), and sassafras (*Sassafras albidum*). If deer density is too high, regeneration of all tree species will fail, including non-oak trees. Active forest management is needed to encourage oak regeneration by keeping oak forests open; ridding the overstory and sub-canopy of non-oak tree species. An increase in exotic invasive understory species can also be anticipated without proper forest management. Proper management can be achieved by cutting and herbicide application of undesired species, which is addressed in this final report. We assume a future deer density of 31–35 per forested sq mi due to the current deer management program, which is a vast improvement over the extraordinarily high deer population (100–200 per forested sq mi) at Valley Forge NHP in the recent past. However, the remaining deer density may still be high enough to interfere with oak regeneration and recruitment, albeit much less severely (Horsley et al. 2003). It is also important to note that controlling deer alone will not facilitate adequate oak regeneration and growth, as it will not impact overstory tree density. Harvesting of overstory trees for the non-target species is needed to keep the forests open and maintain high understory light and low levels of plant competition.

Largay and Sneddon (2007) recommended desired conditions for the Dry Oak Forest and Successional Tuliptree Forest communities at Valley Forge NHP using the framework of the U.S. National Vegetation Classification (USNVC) to write the descriptions and compare existing communities to globally described associations. They identified the desired condition of the Dry Oak Forest as a forest of essentially similar composition to target communities (a Dry Oak Forest on steep slopes with dry, acidic soils and a Dry-Mesic Chestnut Oak Forest on lower slopes with mesic soils) and as having greater ecological integrity than the Successional Tuliptree Forest. The existing Dry Oak Forest type is estimated to have always been present on the ridgetops of Mount Misery and Mount Joy (Largay and Sneddon 2007). Nonetheless, this forest type may be expected to change through the process of forest succession to include more shade-tolerant, non-oak tree species, such as red maple, beech, and blackgum (Abrams 1992). According to Largay and Sneddon (2007), Successional Tuliptree Forest is considered an undesirable type because, as such, it has no known natural or historical analog. These authors propose that the desired condition of the Successional Tuliptree Forest is its conversion to a native Mesophytic Forest type (white oak; *Q. alba*) with high ecological integrity and wildlife value (mast production). It should be noted here that though this report uses the desired forest conditions recommended by Largay and Sneddon (2007), they have not been adopted by the National Park Service as the final target conditions.

2

White-tailed deer, exotic invasive plants, a lack of natural and anthropogenic stand-maintaining disturbance regimes, gypsy moth (*Lymantria dispar*) outbreaks, and abiotic factors such as surrounding land use are among some of the stressors influencing the ecological integrity of the existing Valley Forge NHP forests. Without some form of adaptive management to address the impacts of these stressors, the existing Valley Forge NHP forests are likely to be on successional trajectories with little ecological or historical value. The Largay and Sneddon (2007) report proposes a set of desired conditions and potential target stand metrics for forest communities at Valley Forge NHP, whose mission is to "preserve the cultural and natural resources that commemorate the encampment of the Continental Army at Valley Forge in 1777–78." National Park Service management policies permit the intervention in natural biological or physical processes "to restore natural ecosystem functioning that has been disrupted by past or ongoing human activities." The two directives pose a challenging task that requires finding a suitable balance between the natural and the historical landscape.

Past sampling of Mount Joy and Mount Misery included 30 vegetation sites (15 in each area) established in 1992 (Figure 1; Diefenbach et al. 2008). At each site, paired 2×2-m (6.5×6.5-ft) plots were established where one plot was fenced to exclude deer but no other herbivores, and the other plot was unfenced. A vast majority of tree, shrub, vine, and herbaceous vegetation were identified to species and the number of tree seedlings and non-tree cover were enumerated in all plots; however, this study focused on understory vegetation and has very limited detailed information about the overstory trees, particularly in terms of tree size, density, and basal area needed for forest management plans and implementation of treatments. Eight additional vegetation monitoring plots were sampled in 2000 within the Dry Oak Forest on Mount Misery and five and three additional monitoring plots were sampled in the Dry Oak and Successional Tuliptree forests, respectively, on Mount Joy (Podniesinski et al. 2005). Plot sizes were 20×20 m for forests and woodlands, 10×10 m for shrublands, and 5×5 m for herbaceous vegetation. However, the sampling intensity renders these plots and corresponding data of limited value to detailed forest management decisions. This study also did not include permanently marked plots. Comiskey et al. (2009) included three selected vegetation sampling 20×20-m plots in the Dry Oak Forest and one in the Successional Tuliptree Forest on Mount Misery and one plot in each forest type on Mount Joy. Again, this represents too low of a sampling intensity for forest management purposes.

The study described in this report provides additional vegetation sampling research and results for Valley Forge NHP as a prelude to making proper management recommendations and prescriptions to achieve the desired conditions (according to Largay and Sneddon 2007) in the Dry Oak Forest on Mount Misery and the Dry Oak and Successional Tuliptree forests on Mount Joy.

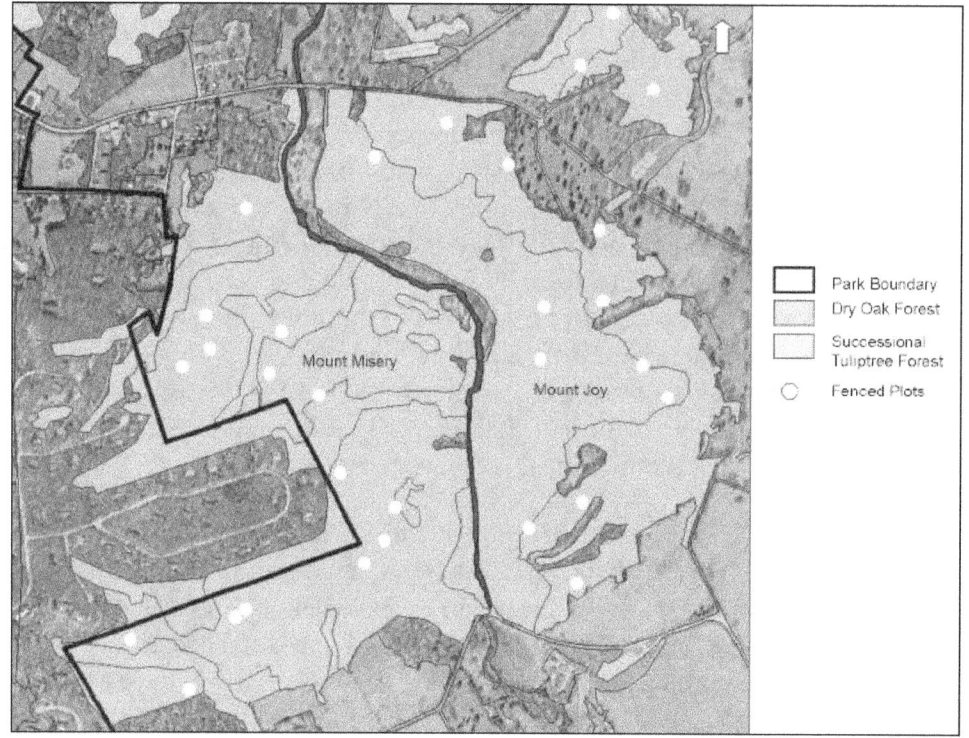

Figure 1. Location of 2×2-m fenced monitoring plots within the Dry Oak Forest and Successional Tuliptree Forest on Mount Misery and Mount Joy, Valley Forge National Historical Park, PA (from Diefenbach et al. 2008). The unfenced plots were located within 20 m of the fenced plots.

Study Objectives

The thirty paired 2×2-m vegetation plots (15 in each area of Mount Joy and Mount Misery) established in 1992 and described in Diefenbach et al. (2008) were resurveyed. The plots were resurveyed for number of tree seedlings (by height class) and saplings, and percent cover of shrub, vine, and herbaceous vegetation by species.

Collection and analyses of new overstory and understory vegetation data in twenty 20×20-m permanently marked plots were conducted in each of the two Dry Oak Forest stands on Mount Misery and Mount Joy and the one Successional Tuliptree Forest on Mount Joy (see Methods). The 20 plots per stand (60 total) were co-located (when appropriate and possible to do so) with the 15 existing 2×2-m unfenced long-term vegetation monitoring plots in the Dry Oak Forest on Mount Misery and the 15 existing 2×2-m unfenced vegetation plots in the two forest types on Mount Joy (including a small patch of forest to the immediate northeast of Mount Joy; Figure 1). The protocol for the newly established 20×20-m plots (using the center point of the 2×2-m plots) followed Comiskey et al. (2009).

This report includes: (1) the monitoring protocol and timing for future data collection; (2) understory vegetation trends over time (1992–2010) for the 30 paired 2×2-m fenced and unfenced plots; (3) understory and overstory vegetation data from the sixty 20×20-m plots; (4) management prescriptions to close the gap between existing and desired forest conditions (based on Largay and Sneddon [2007]); (5) minimum management prescriptions considered necessary (assuming deer densities of 31–35 deer per forested sq mi) to promote tree regeneration regardless of species composition; and (6) successional trajectory in the absence of active forest management.

Study Area Description

Valley Forge National Historical Park (NHP) is located 20 km northwest of Philadelphia, in Chester and Montgomery counties, within the Upland Piedmont Plateau ecological region in southeastern Pennsylvania. The park consists of 1,403 ha (3,466 ac) and is located just south of the boundary between the Glaciated and Piedmont sections of the Oak-Chestnut Forest Region. The area has a long history of human impacts from forest clearing for encampment during the Revolutionary War (1777–1778), agriculture, industrial use, and development. All of these factors, in addition to the bedrock geology, soil composition, and site-specific characteristics, such as slope, aspect, and moisture regime, influence the current-day vegetation patterns at Valley Forge NHP (Rhoads et al. 1989, Podniesinski et al. 2005).

Within Valley Forge National Historical Park, Mount Misery borders Valley Creek to the west and encompasses approximately 93 ha (229 ac) and Mount Joy borders Valley Creek to the east and encompasses approximately 94 ha (233 ac) (Diefenbach et al. 2008). Mount Misery is dominated by Dry Oak Forest with lesser amounts of Successional Tuliptree Forest embedded within the Dry Oak Forest matrix. In contrast, Mount Joy is dominated by Dry Oak Forest in the western half and Successional Tuliptree Forest in the eastern half (Figure 1). The canopy of the Dry Oak Forest type is dominated by drought-tolerant chestnut oak and black oak with lesser amounts of blackgum and scarlet oak. The subcanopy is characterized by moderate-to-dense cover of blackgum, red maple, and sassafras. A tall shrub layer is often diagnostic for this community type and is characterized by moderate to dense cover of mountain laurel. In some stands, the tall-shrub layer is dominated by young blackgum. Also common in the tall-shrub layer are red maple, sassafras, and witch-hazel (*Hamamelis virginiana*). The low-shrub and herbaceous layers are typically very sparse or absent, largely due to heavy deer browse (Largay and Sneddon 2007).

The Successional Tuliptree Forest community comprises tuliptree (*Liriodendron tulipifera*) as the only dominant in many stands, with black oak and white ash as codominant or subdominant trees (Largay and Sneddon 2007). Other occasional canopy trees include red maple, northern red oak (*Q. rubra*), and sassafras. The subcanopy is usually open, characterized by tuliptree, red maple, tall individuals of flowering dogwood (*Cornus florida*), blackgum, occasional redbud (*Cercis canadensis*), and sassafras. Typical tall shrubs include flowering dogwood, witch-hazel, and mountain laurel. The tall-shrub layer varies from sparse to abundant; with flowering dogwood exceeding 50% cover in some locations. The low-shrub and herbaceous layers are very sparse to nearly absent, largely the result of intense deer browse (Largay and Sneddon 2007).

Methods

In 2010, two separate surveys for vegetation sampling and monitoring were conducted during the spring (April 10–19; for spring flora only) and mid-summer (July 10–16) in the 30 paired 2×2-m fenced and unfenced long-term, understory monitoring plots. In addition, the sixty 20×20-m overstory and understory plots were established and monitored in mid-summer in the three study forests on Mount Misery (one Dry Oak Forest) and Mount Joy (one Dry Oak Forest and one Successional Tuliptree Forest); a total of 20 overstory plots per stand. The 60 plots were co-located (when appropriate and possible to do so) with the 15 existing 2×2-m unfenced long-term vegetation monitoring plots in the Dry Oak Forest on Mount Misery and 15 existing 2×2-m unfenced vegetation plots in both forest types on Mount Joy (including a small patch of forest to the immediate northeast of Mount Joy; Figure 1). In the Successional Tuliptree Forest on Mount Joy, five 20×20-m plots were co-located with existing 2×2-m unfenced plots. In the Dry Oak Forest on Mount Joy, four plots were co-located, and in the Dry Oak Forest on Mount Misery, ten plots were co-located. The newly established 20×20-m plots (those that were not co-located with the existing 2×2-m unfenced understory plots; 15 in the Successional Tuliptree Forest, 16 in the Dry Oak Forest on Mount Joy, and ten in the Dry Oak Forest on Mount Misery) were randomly established along transects through the middle of the three forest stands (minimum 20-m distance from roads, trails, and stand boundaries to avoid edge effects). Twenty plots per stand are the "industry standard" in forest ecology and management and are highly appropriate in this study due to the large size of the two study areas (approximately 230 ac each). On Mount Misery, plot locations were restricted to the Dry Oak Forest (excluding the embedded areas of Successional Tuliptree Forest). The plot design of Comiskey et al. (2009) was used to inventory all overstory tree species and understory woody and herbaceous vegetation (Figure 2). When these plots were co-located with the 2×2-m unfenced understory plots, the center of the plot was used as the center of the 20×20-m overstory plot.

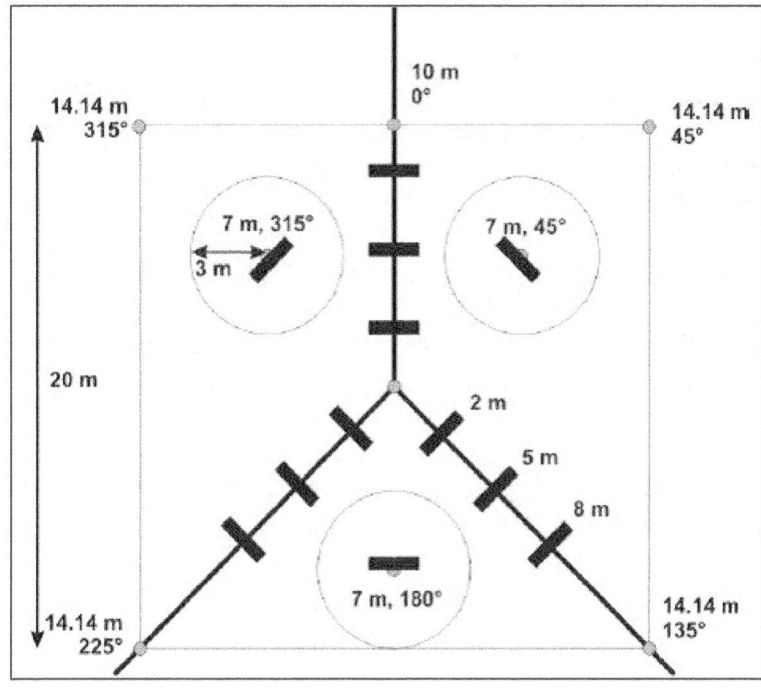

Figure 2. Plot layout showing square tree plot with three nested 3-m radius regeneration microplots and twelve 1-m² vegetation quadrats along the central triad (Comiskey et al. 2009).

2010 Sampling Protocol in the 20×20-m Plots

Within the 20×20-m plots, tree species (classified according to FIA specifications), diameter, and crown class were recorded for all trees ≥ 10.0 cm dbh (diameter at breast height). Classification of tree crowns into four categories (dominant, codominant, intermediate, and overtopped) was based on canopy position and the amount and direction of intercepted light. Overstory trees receiving full light above and partial light on the sides were considered dominant; those receiving full light above and comparatively little on the sides were considered co-dominant; those receiving little direct light from above and none on the sides were classed as intermediate; and those receiving no direct light at all were classed as overtopped. Tree saplings ≥ 1.5 m in height and ≥ 1.0 cm and <10.0 cm dbh were measured in three permanently marked 3-m radius circular micro-plots embedded at each of the 20 sample points (Figure 2). Tree seedlings >5 cm tall and <1 cm dbh were identified in twelve 1-m^2 quadrats, counted, and assigned to height classes of 5–15 cm, 15.1–30 cm, 30.1–100 cm, 100.1–150 cm, and >1.5m. Shrub and herbaceous species were monitored within twelve 1-m^2 quadrats (Figure 2), and the cover of each species was estimated into cover classes (0–4%, 5–25%, 26–50%, 51–75%, 76–95%, and 96–100%). These cover classes were dictated by the Valley Forge NHP park management, although they do vary slightly from Comiskey et al. (2009). All shrub species (classified according to FIA specifications) were assigned into a maximum height class as a whole for each plot. The height classes used for shrub species were the same as the height classes used for tree seedlings. The center of each 20×20-m plot was permanently marked with a metal stake and the centers of the three 3-m radius circular micro-plots were marked with a PVC stake.

2010 Sampling Protocol in the 2×2-m Plots

The 30 paired 2×2-m plots (15 in Mount Joy and 15 in Mount Misery) established in 1992 (described in Diefenbach et al. 2008) were resurveyed using a protocol similar to previous surveys as follows (differences in protocol from previous surveys are noted below):

1. Sampling was done in one centrally located 2×2-m plot (as opposed to four 1×1-m plots used in 2003).

2. All tree seedlings in each vegetation plot were identified to species, counted, and recorded by height class. Tree seedling height classes are defined as follows: 1=5–15 cm, 2=15.1–30 cm, 3=30.1–100 cm, 4=100.1–150 cm, and 5=>1.5 m (this follows Comiskey et al. 2009, but differs from Diefenbach et al. 2008 to better differentiate between short, moderate, and tall seedlings).

3. All shrub species in each plot were identified to species, given a cover class (0–4%, 5–25%, 26–50%, 51–75%, 76–95%, and 96–100%), and assigned a maximum height class based on the tallest individual of each species in each plot; shrub maximum height classes are defined as follows: 5–15 cm, 15.1–30 cm, 30.1–100 cm, 100–150 cm, and >1.5 m.

4. All herbaceous species in each plot were identified to species (with the exception of a few identified to genus) and assigned a cover class: 0–4%, 5–25%, 26–50%, 51–75%, 76–95%, and 96–100%.

In co-located plots, tree seedlings and shrub and herbaceous species were measured using both survey methods.

The classification of vegetative species as herbaceous, vine, or shrub was based on Rhoads and Klein (1993). Additional references were used to confirm species classifications and update taxonomy: Pennsylvania Flora Project database (http://www.paflora.org/), U.S. Department of Agriculture PLANTS database (http://plants.usda.gov/index.html), and the U.S. Department of Agriculture ITIS database (http://www.itis.usda.gov/advanced_search.html).

1993–2003 Sampling Protocols in the 2×2-m Plots (from Diefenbach et al. 2008)

Herbaceous, Shrub, and Vine Cover: 1993 and 1995
Herbaceous vegetation, shrubs, and vines were typically identified to species, and minimally to genus. For each species, a visual estimate of percent cover within a plot was recorded in the following classes: 1=0–4%; 2=5–25%; 3=26–50%; 4=51–75%; 5=76–95%; and 6=96–100%. Vegetation was not stratified by height.

Herbaceous, Shrub, and Vine Cover: 1998
Data were collected as in 1993 and 1995. In addition, each 2×2-m (6.5×6.5-ft) plot was divided into four 1×1-m (3.25×3.25-ft) quadrants in 1998 and at the center of each quadrant mean height of all herbaceous, shrub, and vine species combined was estimated. A visual estimate of percent vegetation cover (all herbaceous, shrub, and vine species combined) within each 2×2-m (6.5×6.5-ft) sample plot also was recorded. All plants in 1998 were identified to species.

Herbaceous, Shrub, and Vine Cover: 2003
Data were collected as in 1993 and 1995. In addition, when it was easy to determine that shrub stems were present within one height class, the height class of shrubs was recorded using the same height classes used for tree seedlings (1=0–25 cm, 2=26–50 cm, 3=51–75 cm, 4=76–100 cm, 5=101–125 cm, and 6=126–150 cm). When shrubs were distributed through multiple height classes, the height of the majority of the shrub cover was recorded in one of the following two height classes, ≤100 cm (≤39.4 in) or >100–150 cm (>39.4–59.0 in).

Tree seedlings: 1993, 1995, 1998, and 2003
All tree seedlings in each 2×2-m (6.5×6.5-ft) vegetation plot were identified to species (except hickory species in 1998), counted, and recorded by height class. Tree seedling height classes were defined as follows: 1=0–25 cm (0–9.8 in); 2=26–50 cm (10.2–19.7 in); 3=51–75 cm (20.0–29.5 in); 4=76–100 cm (29.9–39.4 in); 5=101–125 cm (39.7–49.2 in); and 6=126–150 cm (49.6–59.0 in).

Calculation of Stocking Rates
The desired overstory component species for each forest type were obtained from Largay and Sneddon (2007, Table 1). We calculated stocking rates of these species for only the area within the 2×2-m fenced plots. In the final stocking tables, the desired overstory component species for Dry Oak Forest and Dry-Mesic Chestnut Oak Forest types (the desired forest types for the current Dry Oak Forest) were combined to include all the listed desired species from both types. Stocking rates were calculated for these species for the whole of the Mount Joy and Mount Misery Dry Oak Forest stands (n=22 fenced plots). Even though the desired Dry-Mesic Chestnut Oak Forest is the only type of the two where any of the hickories are important, it is useful to

Table 1. Desired canopy and subcanopy tree species of the Dry Oak (and Dry-Mesic Chestnut Oak) and Mesophytic desired forest types, in order by desired percentage in the canopy, on Mount Joy and Mount Misery, Valley Forge National Historical Park, PA (Largay and Sneddon 2007).

Forest type	Canopy	Subcanopy
Dry Oak Forest	chestnut oak	red maple
	black oak	blackgum
	northern red oak	flowering dogwood
	tuliptree	
	white oak	
	scarlet oak	
	American chestnut	
	pignut hickory	
	mockernut hickory	
	shagbark hickory	
Mesophytic Forest	tuliptree	red maple
	northern red oak	white ash
	white oak	American hornbeam
	black oak	flowering dogwood
	American beech	eastern redbut
	American chestnut	black walnut
	shagbark hickory	
	mockernut hickory	
	pignut hickory	
	American basswood	

show that none of the fenced plots in either of the Dry Oak Forest stands are stocked for any hickory (*Carya* spp.) species. The Mesophytic Forest type is the desired type for the area of Mount Joy currently occupied by the Successional Tuliptree Forest, so the stocking rates for the desired overstory species of the Mesophytic Forest type were calculated based on the data from the fenced plots in the Successional Tuliptree Forest stand (n=8 fenced plots).

We calculated stocking level using weighted seedling counts from the 2010 data. Each seedling was assigned a weight based on height (Table 2), and weighted counts were compiled for plots in the Dry Oak and Successional Tuliptree forest stands. Stem count data collected at Valley Forge National Historical Park in 2010 included only tree species seedlings up to 150 cm in height (as opposed to the weighting system proposed by McWilliams et al. 2002; Table 3) and were recorded in slightly different height classes over the years for the fenced and unfenced plots. We weighted these height classes as closely as possible to those defined by McWilliams et al. (2002),corrected for the different size classes used, and incorporated stocking rates used by Diefenbach et al 2008. Seedlings ≤5.0 cm (≤2 in) in height should not be included in calculating stocking rates because most of these individuals do not survive. We assigned seedlings in the 5.1–15 cm (2.0–5.9 in) class a weight of zero to make it comparable with Diefenbach et al. 2008 (they assigned seedlings less than 25 cm a weight of zero). In addition, we combined the two tallest height classes used by McWilliams et al. (2002) into a single class (>150 cm), represented by saplings recorded in the plots. Guidelines for acceptable abundance of tree seedlings and small saplings for forest regeneration are 25 seedlings per 12.57 m^2 (135.3 ft^2) (McWilliams et al. 2002). With this method of determining regeneration stocking, a weighted score of 25 or more seedlings per 12.57 m^2 (or 19,889 seedlings per ha) is considered adequately stocked. The percentage of plots with adequate seedling abundance is referred to as a stocking rate.

Table 2. Height classes of tree seedlings used at Valley Forge National Historical Park, 2010, and assigned weights for calculating stocking rates of advanced forest regeneration.

Height class	Weight
>5–15 cm	0
>15–30 cm	1
>30–100 cm	2
>100–150 cm	20
>150 cm	50

Table 3. Height classes of tree seedlings and small saplings and assigned weights from U.S. Forest Service, Forest Inventory Analysis (McWilliams et al. 2002), used to calculate stocking rates of advanced forest regeneration.

Height class	Weight
5.1–14.7 cm	1
>14.7–30.0 cm	1
>30–90 cm	2
>90–150 cm	20
>150–310 cm	50
>310 cm and <12.5 cm dbh	50

Calculations of Relative Indices

Data collected on overstory individuals of tree species recorded in the 20×20-m plots were analyzed for frequency, density, dominance, relative frequency, relative density, relative dominance, and relative importance value. The frequency for each tree species is expressed as the number of plots in which overstory individuals of that species occurred. The density of each tree species is the number of overstory individuals of that species found in all plots. Density is then scaled up to the number of trees per ha of each species. Dominance is expressed as the total basal area for overstory individuals of each tree species across all plots, and is also scaled up to basal area (m^2) per ha. Then the relative indices were calculated by dividing each value for each individual species by the column total. Finally, a relative importance value was calculated for each species by adding the relative frequency, relative density, and relative dominance for each tree species and dividing that number by three.

Results

2010 Survey of the 20×20 m Plots

In 2010, twenty 20×20-m plots were surveyed for overstory and understory vegetation in each of the two Dry Oak and one Successional Tuliptree Forest stands on Mount Misery and Mount Joy (Figure 3). In the Successional Tuliptree Forest on Mount Joy, five of these plots were co-located with existing unfenced plots. In the Dry Oak Forest on Mount Joy, four plots were collocated, and in the Dry Oak Forest on Mount Misery, ten plots were co-located.

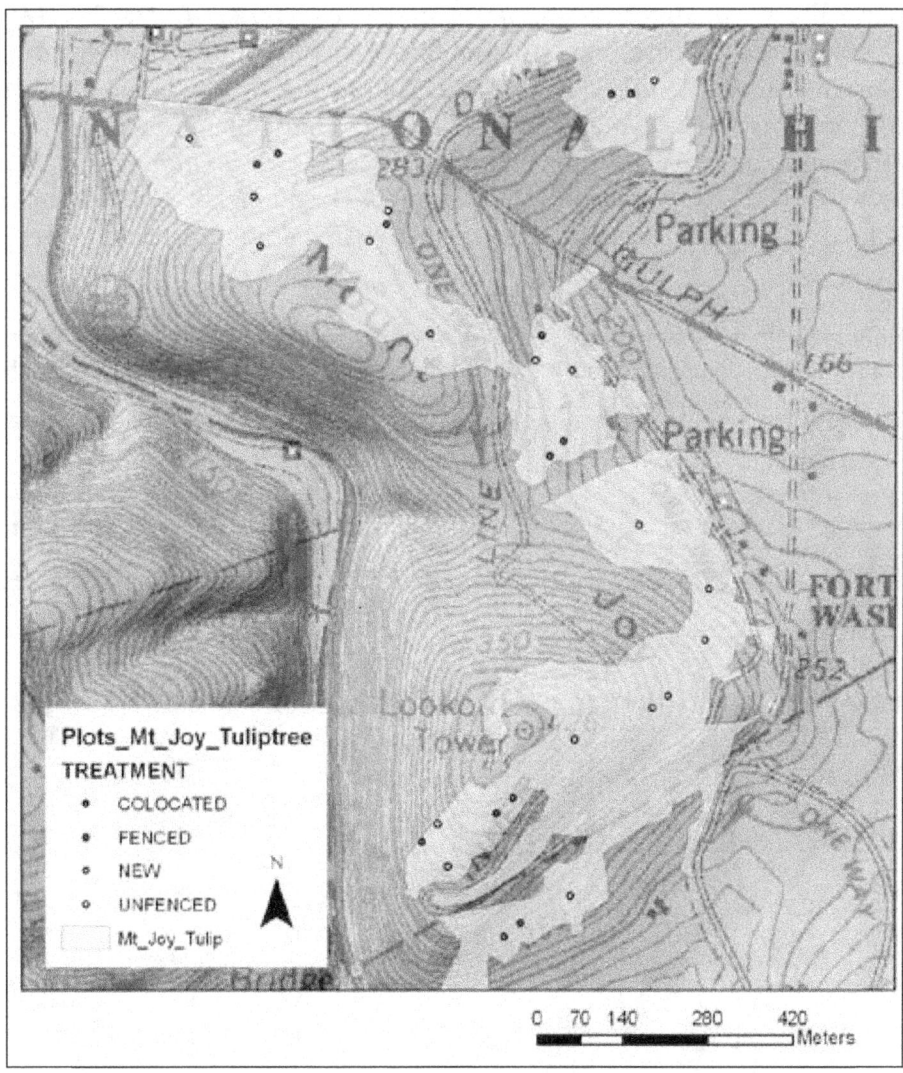

Figure 3. Location of the twenty 20×20-m plots and 2×2-m fenced and unfenced paired plots in the Successional Tuliptree Forest on Mount Joy. Co-located plots refer to the use of a preexisting 2×2-m unfenced plot center for the newly established 20×20-m plot. New plots refer to the newly established 20×20-m plots that were not co-located with the 2×2-m unfenced plots.

15

Successional Tuliptree Forest on Mount Joy

Twenty-one species of trees were recorded in the Successional Tuliptree Forest on Mount Joy (Table 4). The forest was dominated by tuliptree, with a relative importance value of 50.6%. The next closest species were red maple and white ash with relative importance values of 7.5% and 6.5%, respectively. Five oak species were recorded on the site with relative importance values ranging from 0.9 to 3.4%. The only exotic tree species recorded in the stand was tree of heaven (*Ailanthis altissima*).

The diameter distribution for all surveyed trees in the Successional Tuliptree Forest stand on Mount Joy resembles an inverse-J, with more trees in the smaller diameter classes and fewer in the larger classes (Figure 4). Tuliptree dominates all diameter classes from >20–100 cm. The 10–20-cm class has a more even distribution of trees for eight of the surveyed species. Tuliptree also dominated the dominant canopy class in this forest, but shared dominance in the co-dominant canopy class with several other species, including pignut hickory (*C. glabra*), white oak, scarlet oak, northern red oak, black oak, and black locust (*Robinia pseudoacacia*) (Figure 5). Red maple, white pine, Norway maple (*A. platanoides*), and hickory shared dominance in the intermediate canopy class, whereas seven tree species shared dominance in the overtopped class.

Table 4. Frequency (number of plots in which a species occurred), density (trees per ha), dominance (basal area per ha), and relative importance values (%) for all species of trees recorded in the twenty 20×20-m plots in the Successional Tuliptree Forest on Mount Joy, Valley Forge National Historical Park, PA. Relative importance value is the sum of the relative frequency, relative density, and relative dominance divided by three.

Species	Frequency	Density (trees/ha)	Dominance (m^2/ha)	Relative Frequency	Relative Density	Relative Dominance	Relative Importance Value
Liriodendron tulipifera	18	103.75	26.54	27.27	45.60	78.79	50.55
Acer rubrum	8	20.00	0.50	12.12	8.79	1.50	7.47
Fraxinus amemricana	6	13.75	1.45	9.09	6.04	4.32	6.48
Carya tomentosa	4	8.75	0.18	6.06	3.85	0.54	3.48
Nyssa sylvatica	2	15.00	0.23	3.03	6.59	0.67	3.43
Quercus velutina	3	3.75	1.36	4.55	1.65	4.04	3.41
Quercus Montana	3	6.25	0.84	4.55	2.75	2.49	3.26
Cornus florida	3	8.75	0.12	4.55	3.85	0.36	2.92
Prunus avium	2	8.75	0.13	3.03	3.85	0.39	2.42
Quercus alba	2	3.75	0.58	3.03	1.65	1.71	2.13
Acer platanoides	2	6.25	0.19	3.03	2.75	0.56	2.11
Pinus strobus	1	6.25	0.50	1.52	2.75	1.48	1.91
Acer saccharum	2	3.75	0.19	3.03	1.65	0.56	1.74
Prunus serotina	2	3.75	0.06	3.03	1.65	0.19	1.62
Carya glabra	2	2.50	0.24	3.03	1.10	0.71	1.61
Cercis Canadensis	1	3.75	0.04	1.52	1.65	0.11	1.09
Quercus coccinea	1	2.50	0.16	1.52	1.10	0.47	1.03
Ailanthus altissima	1	2.50	0.04	1.52	1.10	0.13	0.91
Quercus rubra	1	1.25	0.19	1.52	0.55	0.57	0.88
Robinia pseudoacacia	1	1.25	0.13	1.52	0.55	0.39	0.82
Celtus occidentalis	1	1.25	0.02	1.52	0.55	0.05	0.71
Total	66	227.5	33.69	100.00	100.00	100.00	100.00

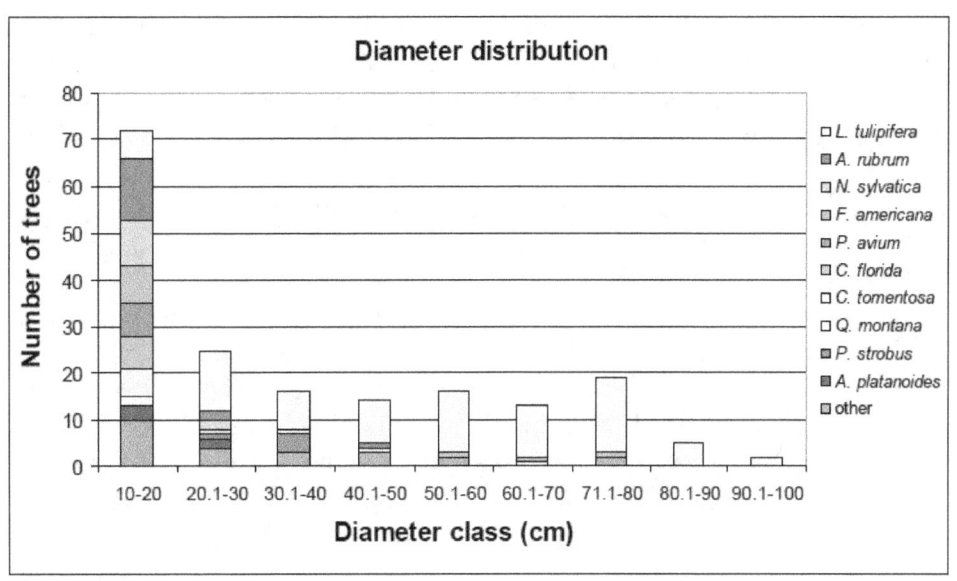

Figure 4. Diameter class distribution for all surveyed trees in the twenty 20×20-m plots for the Successional Tuliptree Forest on Mount Joy, Valley Forge National Historical Park, PA. Other species include: *A. altissima, A. saccharum, C. glabra, C. occidentalis, C. canadensis, P. serotina, Q. alba, Q. coccinea, Q. rubra, Q. velutina,* and *R. pseudoacacia.*

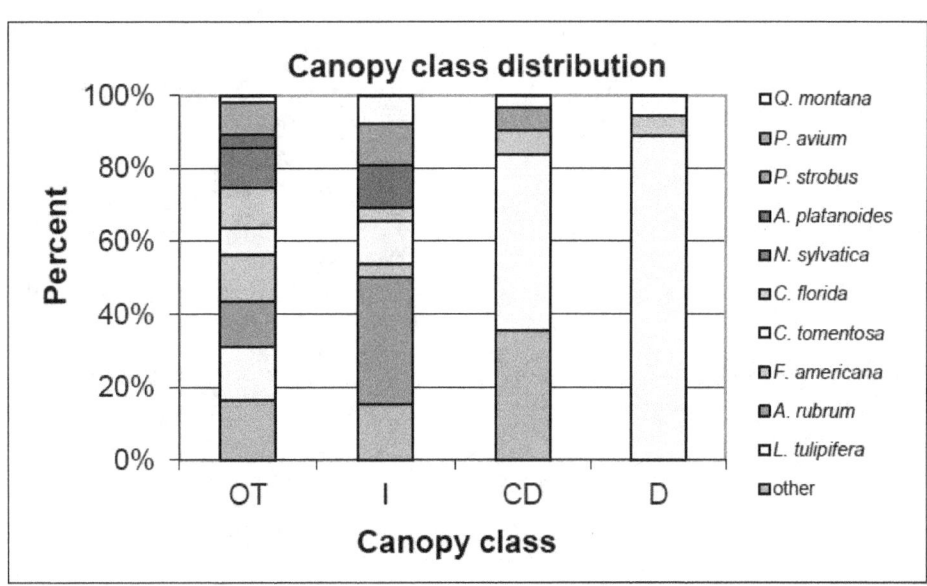

Figure 5. Canopy class distribution for all surveyed trees in the twenty 20×20-m plots for the Successional Tuliptree Forest on Mount Joy, Valley Forge National Historical Park, PA. OT= overtopped (n= 55 trees); I=intermediate (n=26 trees); CD= codominant (n= 31 trees); D= dominant (n=18 trees). Other species include: *A. saccharum, A. altissima, C. canadensis, C. glabra, C. occidentalis, P. serotina, Q. alba, Q. coccinea, Q. rubra, Q. velutina,* and *R. pseudoacacia.*

Ten tree species were recorded as saplings in the Successional Tuliptree Forest stand on Mount Joy, but all occurred at very low density (177 saplings per ha; Table 5). White ash had the highest sapling density at 41.3 per ha, followed by sugar maple (*A. saccharum*), redbud, and flowering dogwood, each with 23.6 saplings per ha. Eight tree species were recorded as seedlings in this stand, with only 3,000 total seedlings per ha (Table 6). Tuliptree and redbud represented most of the recorded seedlings. The average height for most seedlings was 10 cm, which represented the midpoint of the smallest height category used in the study (5–15 cm).

Eight shrub and vine species with an average maximum height of 19 cm were surveyed in the Successional Tuliptree Forest on Mount Joy (Table 7). The cover of these species was extremely low, totaling <1% cover across the stand. Japanese barberry (*Berberis thunbergii*) and spicebush (*Lindera benzoin*) were the tallest of these species. Nineteen herbaceous species were recorded in spring and summer surveys of the 20×20-m plots (Table 8); however, 98% of the total cover was dominated by Japanese stiltgrass (Figure 6).

Table 5. Number and density of tree species saplings recorded in three 3-m radius (28.27 m^2) subplots in each of the twenty 20×20-m plots for the Successional Tuliptree Forest on Mount Joy, Valley Forge National Historical Park, PA.

Species	Count	Saplings/ha
Fraxinus americana	7	41.3
Acer saccharum	4	23.6
Cercis canadensis	4	23.6
Cornus florida	4	23.6
Nyssa sylvatica	3	17.7
Viburnum prunifolium	3	17.7
Acer rubrum	2	11.8
Carya cordiformis	1	5.9
Carya tomentosa	1	5.9
Lindera benzoin	1	5.9
Total	30	176.8

Table 6. Density and mean height of tree species seedlings (with standard error) recorded in twelve 1-m^2 microplots in each of the twenty 20×20-m plots for the Successional Tuliptree Forest on Mount Joy, Valley Forge National Historical Park, PA.

Species	Seedlings/ha	Mean Ht (cm)
Liriodendron tulipifera	1,125.0	10.0±0.0
Cercis canadensis	916.7	10.6±0.6
Sassafras albidum	333.3	10.0±0.0
Nyssa sylvatica	250.0	12.1±2.1
Prunus serotina	166.7	10.0±0.0
Acer rubrum	125.0	10.0±0.0
Prunus virginiana	41.7	10.0±0.0
Carya glabra	41.7	10.0±0.0
Total or Mean	3,000.0	10.4±0.3

Table 7. Percent cover and mean maximum height of shrubs and vines (with standard error) recorded in twelve 1-m² microplots in each of the twenty 20×20-m plots for the Successional Tuliptree Forest on Mount Joy, Valley Forge National Historical Park, PA.

Species	Cover %	Mean Max. Ht.
*Parthenocissus quinquefolia	0.25	8.8±0.5
*Toxicodendron radicans	0.19	7.4±0.8
Berberis thunbergii	0.13	65.1±0.0
Lindera benzoin	0.08	32.5±16.7
Viburnum prunifolium	0.08	10.0±0.0
Euonymus alata	0.06	7.9±1.4
Hamamelis virginiana	0.01	10.0±0.0
*Vitis spp.	0.01	10.0±0.0
Total or Mean	0.80	19.0±7.2

*indicates a vining species.

Table 8. Percent cover of herbaceous species recorded in twelve 1-m² microplots in each of the twenty 20×20-m plots for the Successional Tuliptree Forest on Mount Joy, Valley Forge National Historical Park, PA.

Species	Cover (%)
Microstegium vimineum	72.17±1.8
Arisaema triphyllum	0.64±0.4
Cardamine impatiens	0.35±1.5
*Allium spp.	0.24±0.0
Polygonum caespitosum	0.21±0.0
Viola spp.	0.09±0.0
*Claytonia virginica	0.05±0.0
Circaea alpine	0.04±0.0
Alliaria petiolata	0.03±0.0
Boehmeria cylindrical	0.03±0.0
Carex spp.	0.01±0.0
Carex pensylvanica	0.01±0.0
Duchesnea indica	0.01±0.0
Sanicula spp.	0.01±0.0
Oxalis stricta	0.01±0.0
*Podophyllum peltatum	0.01±0.0
*Sanguinaria Canadensis	0.01±0.0
*Geranium carolinianum	0.01±0.0
*Veronica hederifolia	0.01±0.0
Total	73.92±3.8

*indicates spring ephemeral species

Figure 6. Japanese stiltgrass dominated understory in the Successional Tuliptree Forest on Mount Joy.

Dry Oak Forest on Mount Joy

Twenty-one species of trees were recorded in the Dry Oak Forest on Mount Joy (Table 9, Figure 7). The five oak species combined represent 39.6% of the relative importance value, with more scarlet oak, black oak, and chestnut oak than red oak or white oak. Other common trees in the stand include blackgum, red maple, tuliptree, and black birch (*B. lenta*). The diameter distribution follows an inverse-J, with the larger diameter classes dominated by the oaks and tuliptree, and smaller diameter classes (10–30 cm) dominated by blackgum, red maple, and black birch (Figure 8). The dominant and codominant canopy classes in this forest are mostly represented by the oaks and tuliptree, whereas the intermediate and overtopped canopy classes are mainly blackgum, red maple, black birch, and sassafras (Figure 9).

Nine tree species were recorded as saplings in the Dry Oak Forest on Mount Joy, but at low density (271.2 saplings per ha; Table 10). Blackgum, followed by red maple, represented most of the saplings present. Nine tree species were recorded as seedlings in this forest, totaling 7,458.3 per ha, with an average height of 10 cm (Table 11). Blackgum, sassafras, and red maple comprised most of the seedlings present. The scarcity of oak saplings and seedlings in this forest is noteworthy.

Thirteen species, comprising only 3.6% total cover, were recorded as shrubs or vines in the Dry Oak Forest on Mount Joy (Table 12). The principal shrub was mountain laurel. Average maximum shrub height was 46.6 cm and the tallest species were spicebush, witch hazel, and mountain laurel. Eight herbaceous species were recorded in the spring and summer surveys in this forest (Table 13). Total herbaceous cover of these species was 10.4%, with Japanese stiltgrass representing nearly all of the cover (Figure 10).

Table 9. Frequency (number of plots in which a species occurred), density (trees per ha), dominance (basal area per ha), and relative importance values (%) for all species of trees recorded in the twenty 20×20 m plots in the Dry Oak Forest on Mount Joy, Valley Forge National Historical Park, PA. Relative importance value is the sum of the relative frequency, relative density, and relative dominance divided by three.

Species	Frequency	Density (trees/ha)	Dominance (m^2/ha)	Relative Frequency	Relative Density	Relative Dominance	Relative Importance Value
Nyssa sylvatica	15	105.00	2.67	12.82	24.85	9.64	15.77
Acer rubrum	14	76.25	2.01	11.97	18.05	7.25	12.42
Quercus coccinea	10	31.25	5.31	8.55	7.40	19.18	11.71
Quercus velutina	11	22.50	4.98	9.40	5.33	17.98	10.90
Quercus montana	12	37.50	2.94	10.26	8.88	10.61	9.92
Liriodendron tulipifera	11	31.25	3.42	9.40	7.40	12.35	9.72
Betula lenta	6	35.00	1.72	5.13	8.28	6.22	6.55
Quercus rubra	6	12.50	1.54	5.13	2.96	5.57	4.55
Sassafras albidum	7	23.75	0.41	5.98	5.62	1.48	4.36
Quercus alba	4	7.50	0.68	3.42	1.78	2.46	2.55
Pinus strobus	3	6.25	0.55	2.56	1.48	1.99	2.01
Prunus serotina	4	8.75	0.12	3.42	2.07	0.43	1.97
Fagus grandifolia	2	6.25	0.50	1.71	1.48	1.81	1.66
Fraxinus Americana	3	5.00	0.11	2.56	1.18	0.39	1.38
Acer platanoides	2	2.50	0.16	1.71	0.59	0.58	0.96
Carya tomentosa	2	2.50	0.09	1.71	0.59	0.33	0.88
Ulmus rubra	1	2.50	0.29	0.85	0.59	1.03	0.83
Cercis canadensis	1	2.50	0.05	0.85	0.59	0.19	0.55
Celtis occidentalis	1	1.25	0.09	0.85	0.30	0.31	0.49
Carya glabra	1	1.25	0.03	0.85	0.30	0.09	0.41
Cornus florida	1	1.25	0.03	0.85	0.30	0.09	0.41
Total	117	422.50	27.71	100.00	100.00	100.00	100.00

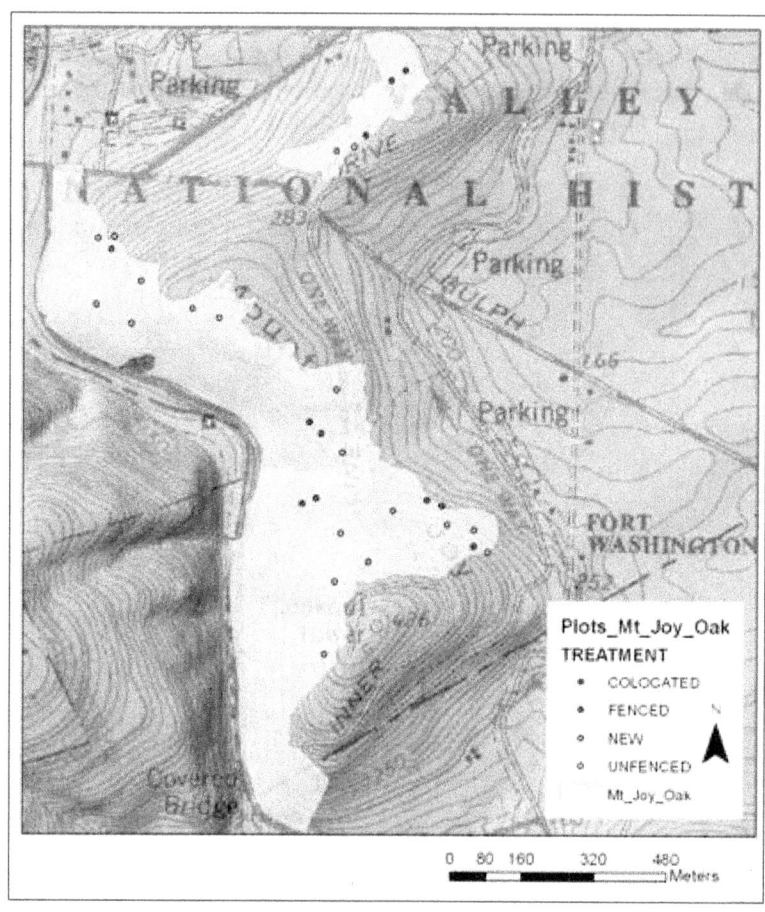

Figure 7. Location of the twenty 20×20-m plots and 2×2-m fenced and unfenced paired plots in the Dry Oak Forest on Mount Joy. Co-located plots refer to the use of a pre-existing 2×2-m unfenced plot center for the newly established 20×20-m plot. New plots refer to newly established 20×20-m plots that were not co-located with the 2×2-m unfenced plots.

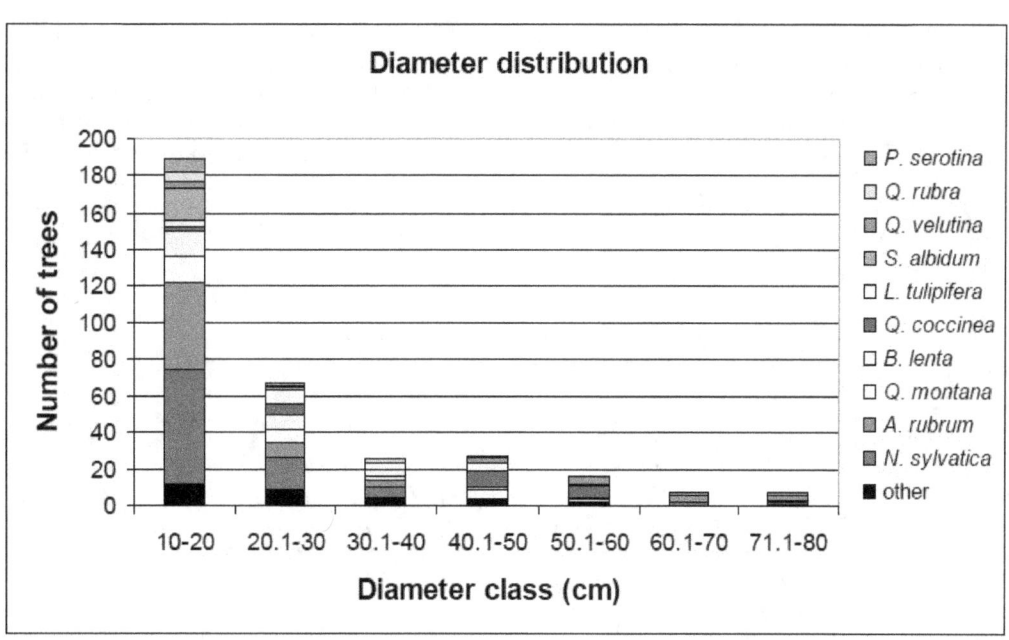

Figure 8. Diameter class distribution for all surveyed trees in the twenty 20×20-m plots for the Dry Oak Forest on Mount Joy, Valley Forge National Historical Park, PA. Other species include: *A. platanoides, C. glabra, C. tomentosa, C. occidentalis, C. canadensis, C. florida, F. grandifolia, F. Americana, P. strobus, Q. alba,* and *U. rubra.*

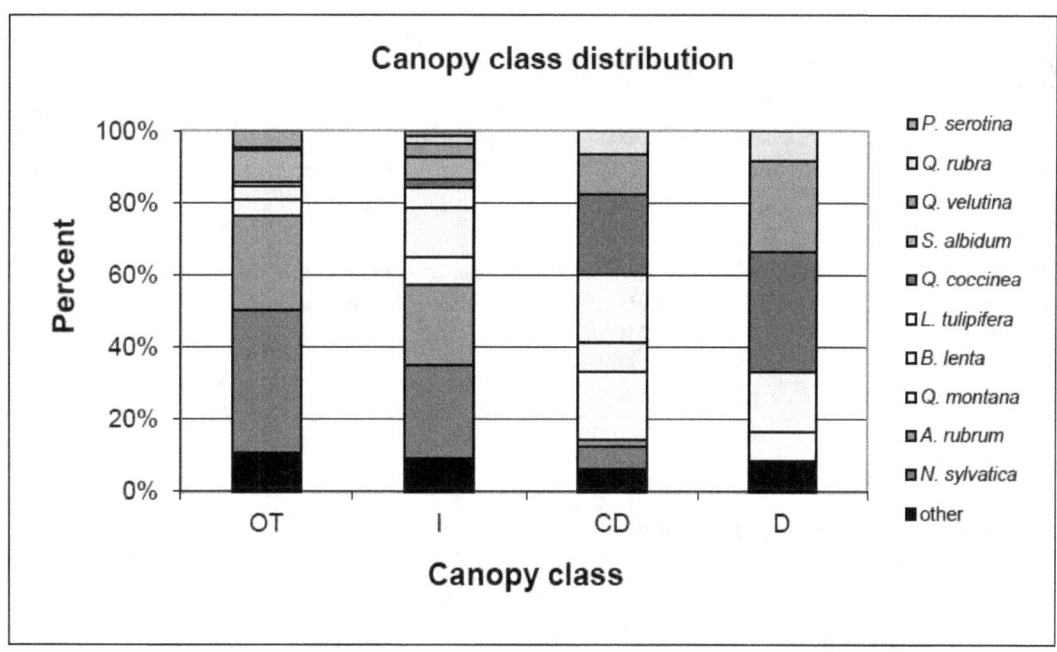

Figure 9. Canopy class distribution for all surveyed trees in the twenty 20×20 m plots for the Dry Oak Forest on Mount Joy, Valley Forge National Historical Park, PA. OT= overtopped (n= 111 trees); I=intermediate (n= 140 trees); CD= codominant (n= 63 trees); D= dominant (n= 24 trees). Other species include: *A. platanoides, C. glabra, C. tomentosa, C. occidentalis, C. canadensis, C. florida, F. grandifolia, F. americana, P. strobus, Q. alba,* and *U. rubra.*

Table 10. Number and density of tree species saplings recorded in three 3-m radius (28.27 m^2) subplots in each of the twenty 20×20-m plots for the Dry Oak Forest on Mount Joy, Valley Forge National Historical Park, PA.

Species	Count	Saplings/ha
Nyssa sylvatica	25	147.4
Acer rubrum	9	53.1
Sassafras albidum	4	23.6
Prunus serotina	3	17.7
Cornus florida	1	5.9
Fraxinus americana	1	5.9
Hamamelis virginiana	1	5.9
Pinus strobus	1	5.9
Quercus coccinea	1	5.9
Total	46	271.2

Table 11. Density and mean height of tree species seedlings (with standard error) recorded in twelve 1-m^2 microplots in each of the twenty 20×20 m plots for the Dry Oak Forest on Mount Joy, Valley Forge National Historical Park, PA.

Species	Seedlings/ha	Mean Ht (cm)
Nyssa sylvatica	2,916.7	10±0.0
Sassafras albidum	2,541.7	10±0.0
Acer rubrum	1,166.7	10±0.0
Prunus serotina	333.3	10±0.0
Quercus Montana	250.0	10±0.0
Betula lenta	125.0	10±0.0
Quercus velutina	41.7	10±0.0
Fraxinus americana	41.7	10±0.0
Prunus virginiana	41.7	10±0.0
Total or Mean	7,458.3	10±0.0

Table 12. Percent cover and mean maximum height of shrub and vine species (with standard error) recorded in twelve 1-m^2 microplots in each of the twenty 20×20-m plots for the Dry Oak Forest on Mount Joy, Valley Forge National Historical Park, PA.

Species	Cover (%)	Mean Max
Kalmia latifolia	2.43	143.9±6.1
Hamamelis virginiana	0.42	150.0±0.0
*Toxicodendron radicans	0.24	6.3±0.7
*Parthenocissus quinquefolia	0.18	8.6±0.6
Lindera benzoin	0.16	10.0±0.0
Viburnum prunifolium	0.05	10.0±0.0
Euonymus alata	0.03	10.0±0.0
*Lonicera japonica	0.02	10.0±0.0
Viburnum acerifolium	0.02	10.0±0.0
Vaccinium angustifolium	0.01	10.0±0.0
Berberis thunbergii	0.01	65.1±0.0
*Smilax glauca	0.01	10.0±0.0
*Vitis spp.	0.01	22.5±0.0
Total or Mean	3.58	46.6±16.6

*indicates a vining species.

Table 13. Percent cover of herbaceous species recorded in twelve 1-m^2 microplots in each of the twenty 20×20-m plots for the Dry Oak Forest on Mount Joy, Valley Forge National Historical Park, PA.

Species	Cover (%)
Microstegium vimineum	9.97±5.0
Carex spp.	0.13±4.3
Cardamine impatiens	0.12±1.6
Thelypteris noveboracensis	0.07±6.5
Carex pensylvanica	0.03±0.0
Arisaema triphyllum	0.03±0.0
Bartonia virginica	0.02±0.0
Prenanthes altissima	0.01±0.0
Total	10.38±1.2

24

Figure 10. Forest overstory (large chestnut oak in left foreground) and Japanese stiltgrass dominated understory in the Dry Oak Forest on Mount Joy. The lower cover and height of stiltgrass may be due to lower soil fertility (relative to the Successional Tuliptree Forest on Mount Joy).

Dry Oak Forest on Mount Misery

Fourteen tree species were recorded in the twenty 20×20-m plots in the Dry Oak Forest on Mount Misery (Figure 11 and Table 14). Five oak species represented 50.9% of the relative importance value; scarlet oak and chestnut oak represented most of this total. Other important trees in the stand include blackgum, red maple, and tuliptree. The inverse-J diameter distribution of trees in this stand contained mostly oaks and tuliptree in the larger and intermediate diameter classes and blackgum and red maple in the smallest class (10–20 cm; Figure 12). Similarly, the canopy class distribution revealed mostly oaks and tuliptree in the dominant and codominant classes, and blackgum and red maple in the intermediate and overtopped classes (Figure 13).

Nine tree species were represented among the 442.1 saplings per ha in the Dry Oak Forest on Mount Misery (Table 15). Blackgum and red maple represented 72% of these saplings. Eight tree species were surveyed among the 7,666.7 seedlings per ha and were primarily blackgum, sassafras, and red maple (Table 16). More oak seedlings (mainly chestnut oak; 875.0 per ha) were recorded here than in the other two forests (excluding the fenced plots).

Nine shrub and vine species with a total cover of only 9.3% were recorded in the Dry Oak Forest on Mount Misery (Table 17). The dominant and tallest shrub was mountain laurel, representing 94% of total cover with a mean maximum height of 147.0 cm. Average height of other species ranged from 7.0–32.0 cm. Six herbaceous species were recorded in the Dry Oak Forest during the spring and summer, but with very minimal cover (0.3% total; Table 18 and Figure 14).

26

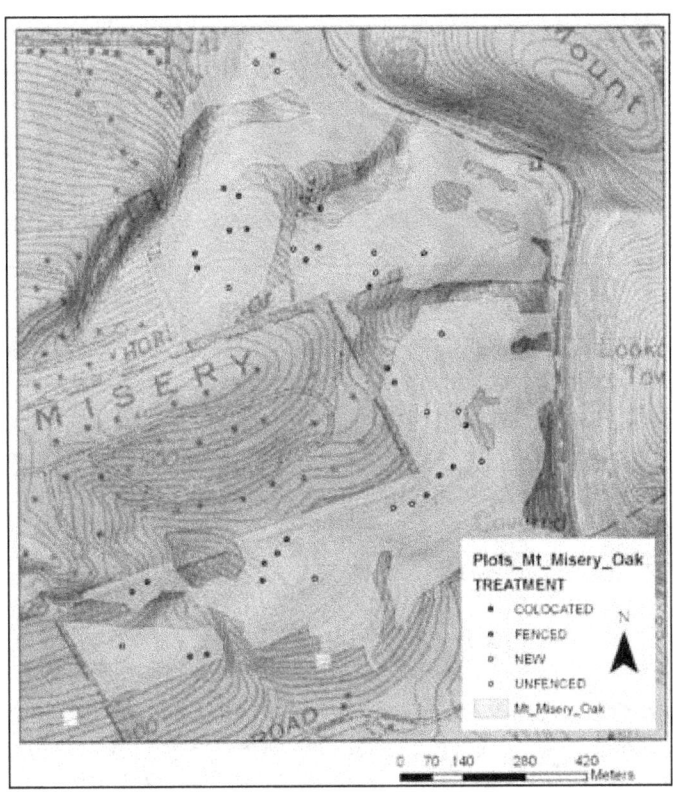

Figure 11. Location of the twenty 20×20-m plots and 2×2-m fenced and unfenced paired plots in the Dry Oak Forest on Mount Misery. Co-located plots refer to the use of a preexisting 2×2-m unfenced plot center for the newly established 20×20-m. New plots refer to the newly established 20×20-m plots that were not co-located with the 2×2-m unfenced plots.

Table 14. Frequency (number of plots in which a species occurred), density (trees per ha), dominance (basal area per ha), and relative importance values (%) for all species of trees recorded in the twenty 20×20-m plots for the Dry Oak Forest on Mount Misery, Valley Forge National Historical Park, PA. Relative importance value is the sum of the relative frequency, relative density, and relative dominance divided by three.

Species	Frequency	Density (trees/ha)	Dominance (m^2/ha)	Relative Frequency	Relative Density	Relative Dominance	Relative Importance Value
Quercus coccinea	17	66.25	9.31	14.29	13.95	29.70	19.31
Quercus montana	18	78.75	8.00	15.13	16.58	25.52	19.08
Nyssa sylvatica	15	112.50	2.21	12.61	23.68	7.06	14.45
Acer rubrum	18	97.50	1.92	15.13	20.53	6.12	13.92
Liriodendron tulipifera	12	38.75	4.10	10.08	8.16	13.07	10.44
Quercus velutina	10	16.25	3.28	8.40	3.42	10.46	7.43
Sassafras albidum	9	32.50	0.58	7.56	6.84	1.84	5.42
Quercus alba	6	12.50	0.95	5.04	2.63	3.05	3.57
Fagus grandifolia	5	7.50	0.42	4.20	1.58	1.35	2.38
Quercus rubra	3	3.75	0.41	2.52	0.79	1.31	1.54
Carya tomentosa	2	3.75	0.06	1.68	0.79	0.20	0.89
Betula lenta	2	2.50	0.08	1.68	0.53	0.24	0.82
Castanea dentate	1	1.25	0.01	0.84	0.26	0.04	0.38
Cornus florida	1	1.25	0.01	0.84	0.26	0.04	0.38
Total	119	475.00	31.34	100.00	100.00	100.00	100.00

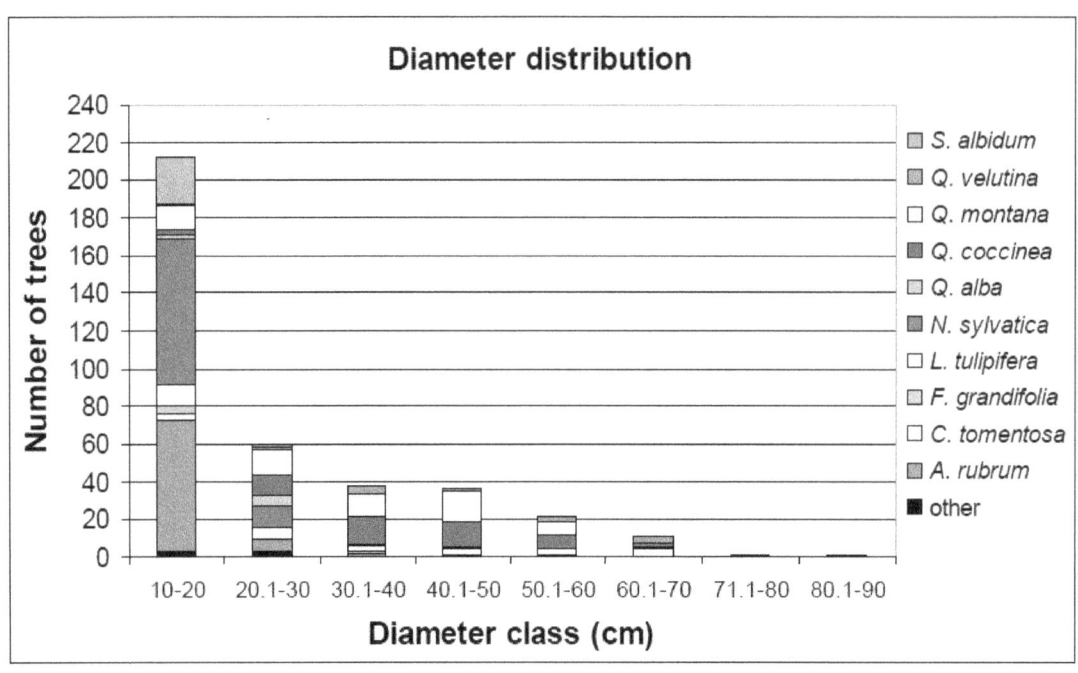

Figure 12. Diameter class distribution for all surveyed trees in the twenty 20×20 m plots for the Dry Oak Forest on Mount Misery, Valley Forge National Historical Park, PA. Other species include: *B. lenta, C. dentata, C. florida,* and *Q. rubra.* The tree in the 71.1–80 cm class is a scarlet oak, and the tree in the 80.1–90 cm class is a black oak.

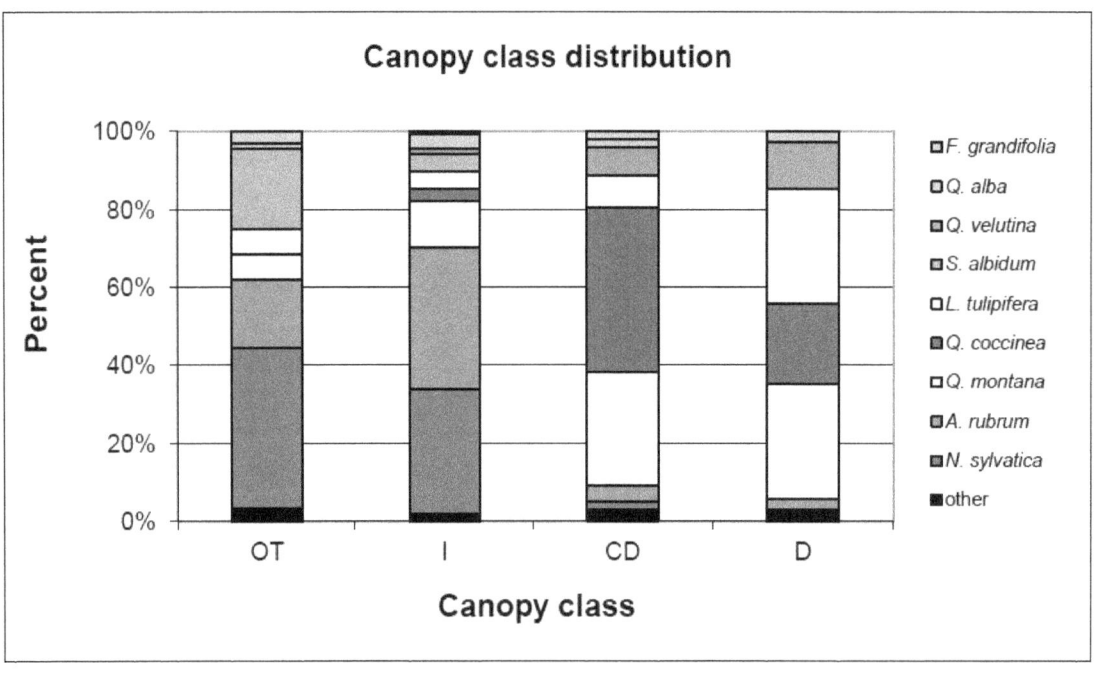

Figure 13. Canopy class distribution for all surveyed trees in the twenty 20×20 m plots for the Dry Oak Forest on Mount Misery, Valley Forge National Historical Park, PA. OT= overtopped (n= 92 trees); I=intermediate (n=157 trees); CD= codominant (n=97 trees); D= dominant (n= 34 trees). Other species include: *B. lenta, C. tomentosa, C. dentata, C. florida,* and *Q. rubra.*

Table 15. Number and density of tree species saplings recorded in three 3-m radius (28.27 m^2) subplots in each of the twenty 20×20-m plots for the Dry Oak Forest on Mount Misery, Valley Forge National Historical Park, PA.

Species	Count	Saplings/ha
Nyssa sylvatica	30	176.8
Acer rubrum	24	141.5
Fagus grandifolia	6	35.4
Liriodendron tulipifera	6	35.4
Sassafras albidum	4	23.6
Carya tomentosa	2	11.8
Acer platanoides	1	5.9
Hamamelis virginiana	1	5.9
Quercus montana	1	5.9
Total	75	442.1

Table 16. Density and mean height of tree species seedlings (with standard error) recorded in twelve 1-m^2 microplots in each of the twenty 20×20-m plots for the Dry Oak Forest on Mount Misery, Valley Forge National Historical Park, PA.

Species	Seedlings/ha	Mean Ht (cm)
Nyssa sylvatica	2,375.0	12.2±0.64
Sassafras albidum	2,333.3	13.0±1.13
Acer rubrum	1,333.3	10.0±0.0
Quercus montana	875.0	10.0±0.0
Prunus serotina	416.7	10.0±0.0
Liriodendron tulipifera	250.0	10.0±0.0
Quercus velutina	41.7	10.0±0.0
Quercus virginiana	41.7	10.0±0.0
Total or Mean	7,666.7	10.7±0.4

Table 17. Percent cover and mean maximum height of shrub and vine species (with standard error) recorded in twelve 1-m^2 microplots in each of the twenty 20×20-m plots for the Dry Oak Forest on Mount Misery, Valley Forge National Historical Park, PA.

Species	Cover (%)	Mean Max Ht (cm)
Kalmia latifolia	8.70	147.0±3.0
Vaccinium angustifolium	0.23	10.0±0.0
Viburnum prunifolium	0.12	10.0±0.0
Hamamelis virginiana	0.06	22.5±0.0
Toxicondendron radicans	0.05	7.5±1.6
Smilax glauca	0.04	32.0±13.5
Parthenocissus quinquefolia	0.04	7.0±1.8
Gaylussacia spp.	0.02	30.1±21.3
Euonymus alata	0.01	10.0±0.0
Total or Mean	9.26	30.7±14.9

*indicates a vining species.

Table 18. Percent cover of herbaceous species recorded in twelve 1-m^2 microplots in each of the twenty 20×20-m plots for the Dry Oak Forest on Mount Misery, Valley Forge National Historical Park, PA.

Species	Cover (%)
Chimaphila maculate	0.12±0.0
Thelypteris noveboracensis	0.07±6.5
Microstegium vimineum	0.03±0.0
Carex pensylvanicia	0.01±0.0
Viola spp.	0.01±0.0
Gaultheria procumbens	0.01±0.0
Total	0.25±0.0

Figure 14. Dry Oak Forest on Mount Misery with very sparse forest understory and apparent deer browse line.

2010 Survey of the 2×2-m Fenced and Unfenced Plots

The thirty 2×2-m paired vegetation plots (15 in each area of Mount Joy and Mount Misery) established in 1992 and described in Diefenbach et al. (2008) were resurveyed in 2010 using a similar protocol to the previous surveys (Figure 15). Eight paired plots are found in the Successional Tuliptree Forest on Mount Joy, seven in the Dry Oak Forest on Mount Joy, and 15 in the Dry Oak Forest on Mount Misery. Nineteen of the unfenced plots in these pairs were co-located with 20×20-m plots; therefore, a small amount of overlap occurs in unfenced plot data. However, these data were analyzed separately for the purpose of comparison with fenced plots, so this overlap is unavoidable.

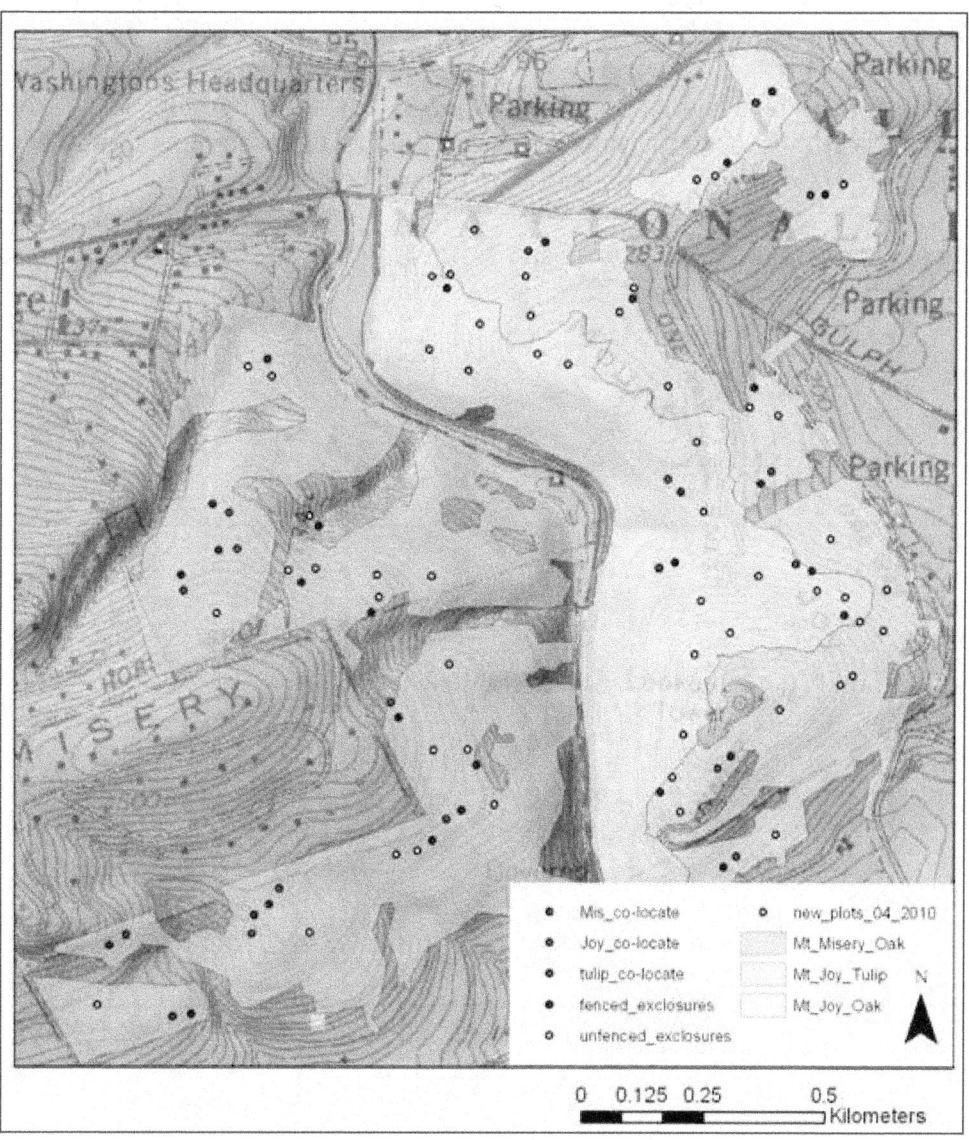

Figure 15. Location of the 2×2-m fenced and unfenced paired plots and twenty 20×20-m plots in the three forests surveyed on Mount Joy and Mount Misery. Co-located plots refer to the use of a preexisting 2×2-m unfenced plot center for a newly established 20×20-m plot. New plots refer to the newly established 20×20-m plots that were not co-located with the 2×2-m unfenced plots.

31

Successional Tuliptree Forest on Mount Joy

In the Successional Tuliptree Forest stand on Mount Joy we recorded 8,437.5 tree species seedlings per ha in the eight fenced plots, compared with only 1,875.0 seedlings per ha in the eight unfenced plots (four are co-located with 20×20-m plots). The only species of tree seedlings in the unfenced plots were red maple, sassafras, and tuliptree, which were also three of the four most common species in the fenced plots (Table 19). Slippery elm (*Ulmus rubra*) was also common in the fenced plots. There were 937.5 chestnut oak and 312.5 red oak seedlings per ha in the fenced plots, and no oak seedlings in the unfenced plots. Total cover of shrub and vine species was 121.5% versus 14.5% in the fenced and unfenced plots, respectively (Table 20). Many of the shrub and vine species were exotic. Indeed, the fenced plots in the Successional Tuliptree Forest on Mount Joy are unique because of the high cover of exotic shrub and vine species. The average height of the shrubs and vines was 101.8 cm in fenced plots and 18.9 cm in unfenced plots. The most common shrub and vine species in the fenced plots were the native spicebush, the exotic European privet (*Ligustrum vulgare*), and honeysuckle (*Lonicera maackii* and *L. japonica*). The most common shrubs and vines in the unfenced plots were the native Virginia creeper (*Parthenocissus quinquefolia*) and blackhaw (*Viburnum prunifolium*) (Table 20). Total cover of herbaceous species was 56.5% (mostly the spring ephemeral mayapple; *Podophyllum peltatum*) in the fenced plots and 71.1% (mostly the exotic Japanese stiltgrass) in the unfenced plots. Japanese stiltgrass cover was very low (0.3%) in the fenced plots (Table 21).

Table 19. Density and mean height of tree species seedlings (with standard error) in the eight fenced and eight unfenced 2×2-m plots in the Successional Tuliptree Forest on Mount Joy, Valley Forge National Historical Park, PA.

Species	Fenced Plots		Unfenced Plots	
	Seedlings/ha	Mean Ht. (cm)	Seedlings/ha	Mean Ht. (cm)
Acer rubrum	1562.5	45.6±12.1	312.5	10.0±0.0
Sassafras albidum	1562.5	10.0±0.0	625.0	10.0±0.0
Ulma rubra	1250.0	54.5±10.7	-	-
Liriodendron tulipifera	937.5	14.2±4.2	937.5	10.0±0.0
Quercus montana	937.5	10.0±0.0	-	-
*Acer platanoides	937.5	18.3±4.2	-	-
Quercus rubra	312.5	10.0±0.0	-	-
Prunus serotina	312.5	65.1±0.0	-	-
Nyssa sylvatica	312.5	65.1±0.0	-	-
Cercis canadensis	312.5	10.0±0.0	-	-
Total or Mean	8,437.5	30.3±7.7	1,875.0	10.0±0.0

*indicates exotic species

Table 20. Shrub and vine cover percentage and mean height (with standard error) in the eight fenced and eight unfenced 2×2-m plots in the Successional Tuliptree Forest on Mount Joy, Valley Forge National Historical Park, PA.

Species	Fenced Plots		Unfenced Plots	
	Cover (%)	Mean Ht. (cm)	Cover (%)	Mean Ht. (cm)
Lindera benzoin	37.75±13.2	110.4±22.1	0.50±0.0	10.0±0.0
*Ligustrum vulgare	17.63±12.6	115.0±35.0	-	-
*Lonicera maackii	17.25±20.6	150.0±0.0	-	-
*Lonicera japonica	14.75±13.4	115.0±35.0	-	-
Viburnam prunifolium	9.50±0.0	150.0±0.0	5.00±18.0	80.0±70.0
*Rosa multiflora	7.88±0.0	150.0±0.0	-	-
*Rhodotypos scandens	4.75±0.0	125.0±0.0	-	-
Viburnum acerifolium	4.75±0.0	125.0±0.0	-	-
*Celastrus orbiculatus	2.38±4.3	141.7±8.3	0.25±0.0	10.0±0.0
*Lonicera morrowii	1.88±0.0	150.0±0.0	-	-
Parthenocissus quinquefolia	1.25±0.0	15.0±3.1	8.00±0.0	10.0±0.0
*Rubus phoenicolasius	0.75±0.0	66.7±33.2	-	-
*Euonymus alata	0.50±0.0	37.6±27.6	0.25±0.0	10.0±0.0
Vitis vulpine	0.25±0.0	65.1±0.0	-	-
Toxicodendron radicans	0.25±0.0	10.0±0.0	0.25±0.0	2.5±0.0
Smilax glauca	-	-	0.25±0.0	10.0±0.0
Total or Mean	121.50	101.8±12.9	14.50	18.9±10.2

Table 21. Herbaceous species cover percentage in the eight fenced and eight unfenced 2×2-m plots in the Successional Tuliptree Forest on Mount Joy, Valley Forge National Historical Park, PA.

Species	Fenced Cover (%)	Unfenced Cover (%)
*Podophyllum peltatum	22.63±12.4	-
Osmorhiza claytoni	6.63±11.5	-
Polygonatum biflorum	5.25±12.0	-
Cimicifuga racemosa	4.00±4.3	-
Circaea alpine	3.13±2.2	-
*Sanguinaria canadensis	2.38±4.3	-
Arisaema triphyllum	2.38±4.3	1.00±0.0
*Claytonia virginica	2.13±6.5	-
Viola spp.	1.88±0.0	0.75±0.0
Polygonum virginianum	1.88±0.0	-
Maianthemum racemosum	0.75±0.0	-
Uvularia perfoliata	0.50±0.0	-
*Geranium carolinianum	0.50±0.0	-
^Alliaria petiolata	0.25±0.0	0.25±0.0
^Microstegium vimineum	0.25±0.0	63.38±13.1
Hepatica nobilis	0.25±0.0	-
Sanicula spp.	0.25±0.0	-
Pteridium aquilinum	0.25±0.0	-
Geum canadense	0.25±0.0	-
Eupatorium purpureum	0.25±0.0	-
*Allium spp.	0.25±0.0	0.25±0.0
^Cardamine impatiens	0.25±0.0	3.75±0.0
Symphyotrichum divaricatum	0.25±0.0	-
^Polygonum caespitosum	-	1.00±0.0
Boehmeria cylindrical	-	0.50±0.0
^Duchesnea indica	-	0.25±0.0
Total	56.50	71.13

*indicates spring ephemeral species
^indicates exotic species

34

Dry Oak Forest on Mount Joy

The seven fenced plots in the Dry Oak Forest stand on Mount Joy contained 36,428.6 seedlings per ha, compared with only 3,214.3 seedlings per ha in the seven unfenced plots (four are co-located with 20×20-m plots; Table 22). Eleven tree species were recorded as seedlings in the fenced plots compared with only three species in the unfenced plots. The most common species of seedlings in the fenced plots were red maple, white ash, and blackgum. There were 2,143 seedlings per ha of oaks and hickory combined. This is compared to nearly 28,000 seedlings per ha of red maple, white ash, and blackgum, combined. In the unfenced plots, blackgum was the dominant species of seedling, with no oak or hickory recorded. The average height of seedlings in the fenced plots was 28.1 cm compared with only 10.0 cm in unfenced plots. Ten shrub and vine species with a total mean cover of 34.7% were recorded in the fenced plots in the Dry Oak Forest on Mount Joy; this compares with only three species with a total mean cover of 3.0% in the unfenced plots (Table 23). The average height of these plants was similar in the fenced (59.0 cm) and unfenced (52.9 cm) plots. Dominant shrub and vine species in the fenced plots were Virginia creeper, blackberry (*Rubus pensylvanicus*), and maple leaf viburnum (*Viburnum acerifolium*). Total herbaceous cover was 16.0% in the fenced plots (mainly garlic mustard [*Alliaria petiolata*] and Solomon's seal [*Polygonatum biflorum*]) and 2.7% in the unfenced plots (Table 24).

Table 22. Density and mean height of tree species seedlings (with standard error) in the seven fenced and seven unfenced 2×2-m plots in the Dry Oak Forest on Mount Joy, Valley Forge National Historical Park, PA.

Species	Fenced Plots		Unfenced Plots	
	Seedlings/ha	Mean Ht. (cm)	Seedlings/ha	Mean Ht. (cm)
Acer rubrum	13,214.3	19.9±3.4	357.1	10±0.0
Fraxinus americana	8,214.3	53.4±9.9	-	-
Nyssa sylvatica	6,428.6	47.5±10.3	2,500.0	10±0.0
Prunus serotina	2,500.0	25.7±10.2	-	-
Sassafras albidum	2,500.0	11.8±1.8	-	-
^*Acer platanoides*	1,071.4	14.2±4.2	-	-
Quercus montana	714.3	16.3±6.3	-	-
Quercus rubra	714.3	65.1±0.0	-	-
Quercus velutina	357.1	22.5±0.0	-	-
Carya glabra	357.1	10.0±0.0	-	-
Betula lenta	357.1	22.5±0.0	-	-
Liriodendron tulipifera	-	-	357.1	10±0.0
Total or Mean	36,428.6	28.1±5.6	3,214.3	10±0.0

^indicates exotic species

Table 23. Shrub and vine cover percentage and mean height (with standard error) in the seven fenced and seven unfenced 2×2-m plots in the Dry Oak Forest on Mount Joy, Valley Forge National Historical Park, PA.

Species	Fenced Plots		Unfenced Plots	
	Cover%	Mean Ht. (cm)	Cover (%)	Mean Ht. (cm)
Parthenocissus quinquefolia	11.7±14.5	16.3±3.6	0.29±0.0	2.5±0.0
Rubus pensilvanicus	8.57±0.0	65.1±0.0	-	-
Viburnum acerifolium	5.71±18.0	43.8±21.3	-	-
Toxicodendron radicans	3.00±3.3	26.9±13.1	0.57±0.0	6.3±3.8
Rhododendron periclymenoides	2.43±6.5	65.1±0.0	-	-
Viburnum prunifolium	2.14±0.0	125.0±0.0	-	-
Vaccinium angustifolium	0.29±0.0	22.5±0.0	-	-
Smilax glauca	0.29±0.0	10.0±0.0	-	-
Phytolacca americana	0.29±0.0	65.1±0.0	-	-
^Celastrus obiculatus	0.29±0.0	150.0±0.0	-	-
Vitis aestivalis	-	-	2.14±0.0	150.0±0.0
Total or Mean	34.71	59.0±14.7	3.00	52.9±48.5

^indicates exotic species

Table 24. Herbaceous species cover percentage in the seven fenced and seven unfenced 2×2-m plots in the Dry Oak Forest on Mount Joy, Valley Forge National Historical Park, PA.

Species	Fenced Cover (%)	Unfenced Cover (%)
^Alliaria petiolata	7.86±10.5	-
Polygonatum biflorum	5.43±0.0	-
Maianthemum racemosum	2.14±0.0	-
^Microstegium vimineum	0.29±0.0	2.71±4.3
Carex swanii	0.29±0.0	-
Total	16.0	2.71

^indicates exotic species

Dry Oak Forest on Mount Misery

The 15 fenced plots in the Dry Oak Forest stand on Mount Misery contained 43,833.3 seedlings per ha, compared to 9,500.0 seedlings per ha in the 15 unfenced plots (ten are co-located with 20×20-m plots; Table 25). Eight tree species were recorded as seedlings in the fenced plots compared with five tree species in the unfenced plots. The most common species of seedlings in the fenced plots were chestnut oak, sassafras, red maple, and blackgum. These same species were common in the unfenced plots, except that sassafras and blackgum had higher densities than chestnut oak and red maple. There were 21,333.4 seedlings per ha of oaks and hickory combined in the fenced plots, compared with only 1,833.3 seedlings per ha for these species in the unfenced plots. The average height of seedlings in the fenced plots was 25.6 cm compared with only 10.0 cm in the unfenced plots.

Sixteen shrub and vine species with a total mean cover of 23.7% were recorded in the fenced plots in the Dry Oak Forest on Mount Misery compared with seven species with a total mean cover of 2.1% in the unfenced plots (Table 26). The average height of these plants was 42.6 cm and 30.4 cm in the fenced and unfenced plots, respectively. Dominant shrub and vine species in the fenced plots were maple leaf viburnum, blueberry (*Vaccinium angustifolium*), mountain laurel, and rhododendron (*Rhododendron periclymenoides*). Total herbaceous cover was 14.3% in the fenced plots (mainly hayscented fern [*Dennstaedtia punctilobula*] and white wood aster [*Symphyotrichum divericatum*]) and 4.1% in the unfenced plots (Table 27).

Table 25. Density and mean height of tree species seedlings (with standard error) in the 15 fenced and 15 unfenced 2×2-m plots in the Dry Oak Forest on Mount Misery, Valley Forge National Historical Park, PA.

Species	Fenced Plots		Unfenced Plots	
	Seedlings/ha	Mean Ht. (cm)	Seedlings/ha	Mean Ht. (cm)
Quercus montana	19,833.3	20.7±1.6	1,833.3	10.0±0.0
Sassafras albidum	9,166.7	32. ±4.1	3,500.0	10.0±0.0
Acer rubrum	6,166.7	15.7±2.1	1,166.7	10.0±0.0
Nyssa syhlvatica	6,166.7	34.8±5.8	2,666.7	10.0±0.0
Quercus velutina	1,166.7	37.2±10.1	-	-
Prunus serotina	1,000.0	19.2±9.2	333.3	10±0.0
Quercus rubra	166.7	22.5±0.0	-	-
Carya tomentosa	166.7	22.5±0.0	-	-
Total or Mean	43,833.3	25.6±2.8	9,500.0	10.0±0.0

Table 26. Shrub and vine cover percentage and mean height (with standard error) in the 15 fenced and 15 unfenced 2×2-m plots in the Dry Oak Forest on Mount Misery, Valley Forge National Historical Park, PA.

Species	Fenced Plots		Unfenced Plots	
	Cover%	Mean Ht. (cm)	Cover (%)	Mean Ht. (cm)
Viburnum acerifolium	5.93±4.9	66.5±17.8	-	-
Vaccinium angustifolium	3.93±2.0	38.3±7.4	0.67±0.0	12.5±2.5
Kalmia latifolia	3.13±3.3	111.9±30.4	0.13±0.0	150.0±0.0
Rhododendron periclymenoides	3.13±3.3	54.5±10.7	-	-
Kalmia angustifolia	2.67±18.0	37.6±27.6	-	-
Gaylussacia frondosa	1.27±4.3	32.5±16.7	-	-
Gaylussacia baccata	1.00±0.0	65.1±0.0	-	-
Viburnum dentatum	1.00±0.0	65.1±0.0	-	-
Smilax glauca	0.40±0.0	14.2±4.2	0.13±0.0	10.0±0.0
Gaylussacia spp.	0.27±0.0	43.8±21.3	-	-
Hamamelis virginiana	0.27±0.0	22.5±0.0	0.13±0.0	10.0±0.0
Parthenocissus quinquefolia	0.13±0.0	22.5±0.0	0.40±0.0	10.0±0.0
Rubus pensilvanicus	0.13±0.0	65.1±0.0	-	-
Toxicodendron radicans	0.13±0.0	10.0±0.0	0.13±0.0	10.0±0.0
Vaccinium stamineum	0.13±0.0	22.5±0.0	-	-
Vitis aestivalis	0.13±0.0	10.0±0.0	-	-
Viburnum prunifolium	-	-	0.53±0.0	10.0±0.0
Total or Mean	23.70	42.6±6.9	2.13	30.4±19.9

Table 27. Herbaceous species cover percentage in the 15 fenced and 15 unfenced 2×2-m plots in the Dry Oak Forest on Mount Misery, Valley Forge National Historical Park, PA.

Species	Fenced Cover (%)	Unfenced Cover (%)
Dennstaedtia punctilobula	6.93±20.0	2.53±0.0
Symphyotrichum divaricatum	2.53±0.0	-
Maianthemum racemosum	1.13±6.5	-
Maianthemum canadense	1.00±0.0	0.13±0.0
Desmodium nudiflorum	1.00±0.0	-
Thelypteris noveboracensis	0.27±0.0	1.00±0.0
Chimaphila maculate	0.27±0.0	0.27±0.0
Aralia nudicaulis	0.27±0.0	-
Polygonatum biflorum	0.13±0.0	-
Uvularia perfoliata	0.13±0.0	-
^Polygonum caespitosum	0.13±0.0	-
Pteridium aquilinum	0.13±0.0	-
Isotria verticillata	0.13±0.0	-
Medeola virginiana	0.13±0.0	-
Prenanthes altissima	0.13±0.0	-
Carex pensylvanica	-	0.13±0.0
Total	14.33	4.07

^indicates exotic species

All Paired Plots Combined

A compilation of the fenced and unfenced data from all 30 paired plots in the three study forests reveal that 15 tree species were recorded as seedlings in the fenced plots, while only six species were in the unfenced plots (Table 28). Fenced plots had a total seedling density of 33,133.2 per ha versus 6,256.7 per ha in the unfenced plots. Chestnut oak seedling density was 10,329.6 per ha in the fenced plots versus 916.7 per ha in the unfenced plots. Seedling densities of red maple and blackgum, two tree species of importance in the understories of all three stands and desired subcanopy components of the Dry Oak Forest type according to Largay and Sneddon (2007), were also higher in the fenced (6,778 per ha and 4,769 per ha, respectively) than unfenced plots (751 per ha and 1,958 per ha, respectively).

A compilation of the fenced and unfenced data from all 30 paired plots in the three study forests reveals that 29 species were recorded as shrubs and vines in the fenced plots, while only 11 species were in the unfenced plots (Table 29; Figure 16). The fenced plots had total shrub and vine cover of 50.9% versus 5.4% in the unfenced plots. The dominant shrubs present in the fenced plots were spicebush and maple leaf viburnum. Thirty-four herbaceous species were recorded in the 30 fenced plots and 14 in the 30 unfenced plots (Table 30). Total herbaceous cover in the fenced plots (25.3%) and unfenced plots (20.5%) was fairly similar. The relatively high herbaceous cover in the unfenced plots, relative to that of shrubs and vines, was due to Japanese stiltgrass, a species avoided by deer.

Although the collection of data for tree-sized ($\geq$10 cm dbh) and sapling-sized ($\geq$ 1.5 m in height, and >1.0 cm and < 10.0 cm dbh) stems of tree species in the 2×2-m fenced and unfenced plots is not part of the long-term survey procedures, we recorded these individuals during the 2010 survey. These data are summarized in Table 31.

Table 28. Compilation of fenced and unfenced tree species seedling densities (all 30 paired plots) in the three forest stands on Mount Joy and Mount Misery, Valley Forge National Historical Park, PA.

Species	Fenced Plots Seedlings/ha	Unfenced Plots Seedlings/ha
Quercus montana	10,329.6	916.7
Acer rubrum	6,777.5	750.7
Sassafras albidum	5,599.0	2,140.6
Nyssa sylvatica	4,768.6	1,958.3
Fraxinus americana	2,053.6	-
Prunus serotina	1,203.1	166.7
Quercus velutina	672.6	-
^Acer platanoides	502.2	-
Quercus rubra	340.0	-
Ulmus rubra	312.5	-
Liriodendron tulipifera	234.4	323.7
Carya glabra	89.3	-
Betula lenta	89.3	-
Carya tomentosa	83.3	-
Cercis Canadensis	78.1	-
Total	**33,133.2**	**6,256.7**

^indicates an exotic species

Table 29. Compilation of fenced and unfenced shrub and vine species percent cover (all 30 paired plots) in the three forest stands on Mount Joy and Mount Misery, Valley Forge National Historical Park, PA.

Species	Fenced Cover (%)	Unfenced Cover (%)
Lindera benzoin	9.44	0.13
Viburnum acerifolium	5.58	-
^Ligustrum vulgare	4.41	-
^Lonicera maackii	4.31	-
^Lonicera japonica	3.69	-
Parthenocissus quinquefolia	3.31	2.27
Viburnum prunifolium	2.91	1.52
Rubus pensilvanicus	2.21	-
Rhododendron periclymenoides	2.17	-
Vaccinium angustifolium	2.04	0.33
^Rosa multiflora	1.97	-
Kalmia latifolia	1.57	0.07
Kalmia angustifolia	1.33	-
^Rhodotypos scandens	1.19	-
Toxicondendron radicans	0.88	0.27
^Celastrus orbiculatus	0.67	0.06
Gaylussacia frondosa	0.63	-
Gaylussacia baccata	0.50	-
Viburnum dentatum	0.50	-
^Lonicera morrowii	0.47	-
Smilax glauca	0.27	0.13
^Rubus phoenicolasius	0.19	-
Gaylussacia spp.	0.13	-
Hamamelis virginiana	0.13	0.07
^Euonymus alata	0.13	0.06
Phytolacca americana	0.07	-
Vitis aestivalis	0.07	0.54
Vaccinium stamineum	0.07	-
Vitis vulpine	0.06	-
Total	**50.89**	**5.44**

Figure 16. A) fenced plot in the Dry Oak Forest on Mount Joy with tree seedlings and shrubs surrounded by Japanese stiltgrass outside of exclosure; B) high density chestnut oak seedlings in fenced plot in Dry Oak Forest on Mount Misery; C) unfenced plot in Dry Oak Forest on Mount Misery devoid of vegetation; and D) dense woody vegetation in fenced plot surrounded by Japanese stiltgrass in the Successional Tuliptree Forest on Mount Joy. Photo descriptions are clockwise from top left.

Table 30. Compilation of fenced and unfenced herbaceous species percentage cover (all 30 paired plots) in the three forest stands on Mount Joy and Mount Misery, Valley Forge National Historical Park, PA.

Species	Fenced Cover (%)	Unfenced Cover (%)
*Podophyllum peltatum	5.66	-
Dennstaedtia punctilobula	3.47	1.27
Polygonatum biflorum	2.74	-
^Alliaria petiolata	2.03	0.06
Osmorhiza claytoni	1.66	-
Symphyotrichum divaricatum	1.33	-
Maianthemum racemosum	1.29	-
Cimicifuga racemosa	1.00	-
Circaea alpine	0.78	-
*Sanguinaria canadensis	0.59	-
Arisaema triphyllum	0.59	0.25
*Claytonia virginica	0.53	-
Maianthemum canadense	0.50	0.07
Desmodium nudiflorum	0.50	-
Viola spp.	0.47	0.19
Polygonum virginianum	0.47	-
Uvularia perfoliata	0.19	-
^Microstegium vimineum	0.13	16.52
Thelypteris noveboracensis	0.13	0.50
Chimaphila maculate	0.13	0.13
Aralia nudicaulis	0.13	-
Pteridium aqualinum	0.13	-
*Geranium carolinianum	0.13	-
Carex swanii	0.07	-
^Polygonum caespitosum	0.07	0.25
Isotria verticillata	0.07	-
Medeola virginiana	0.07	
Prenanthes altissima	0.07	-
Hepatica nobilis	0.06	-
Sanicula spp.	0.06	-
Geum canadense	0.06	-
Eupatorium purpureum	0.06	-
*Allium spp.	0.06	0.06
^Cardamine impatiens	0.06	0.94
Boehmeria cylindrical	-	0.13
^Duchesnea indica	-	0.06
Carex pensylvanica	-	0.07
TOTAL	25.29	20.49

*Indicates spring ephemeral species
^Indicates exotic species

Table 31. Number of sapling stems and dbh of individual tree-sized stems of tree species in the 2×2-m fenced and unfenced plots on Mount Joy and Mount Misery, Valley Forge National Historical Park, PA.

Species	Plot	Sapling Count	Tree-sized dbh (cm)
Mount Joy Successional Tuliptree Forest			
Acer rubrum	J18 Fenced	2	-
Nyssa sylvatica	J18 unfenced	1	-
Sassafras albidum	J18 Unfences	-	10.7
Prunus serotina	J19 Fenced	1	-
Mount Joy Dry Oak			
Fraxinus americana	J22 Fenced	1	-
Acer rubrum	J23 Fenced	1	-
^Acer platanoides	J23 Fenced	2	-
Nyssa sylvatica	J26 Fenced	1	-
Nyssa sylvatica	J26 Unfenced	-	13.0
Mount Misery Dry Oak Forest			
Nyssa sylvatica	M03 Fenced	1	-
Nyssa sylvatica	M03 Unfenced	1	-
Nyssa sylvatica	M05 Fenced	2	-
Nyssa sylvatica	M05 Unfenced	1	-
Liriodendron tulipifera	M06 Fenced	1	-
Liriodendron tulipifera	M06 Fenced	-	21.6
Liriodendron tulipifera	M06 Unfenced	1	-
Nyssa sylvatica	M07 Unfenced	-	11.9
Sassafras albidum	M13 Fenced	1	-
Acer rubrum	M15 Fenced	1	-
Acer rubrum	M15 Fenced	-	21.6

1993–2010 Surveys of the 2×2-m Fenced and Unfenced Plots

Between 1993 and 2010, the average number of plant species (woody and herbaceous) per plot decreased in the 2×2-m unfenced plots, but remained fairly constant in the fenced plots, on Mount Joy and Mount Misery (Table 32).

Table 32. Average number (richness) of woody and herbaceous species combined per plot in the 2×2-m fenced and unfenced plots on Mount Misery and Mount Joy, Valley Forge National Historical Park, PA, 1993–2010.

Year	Mount Misery				Mount Joy			
	Fenced		Unfenced		Fenced		Unfenced	
1993	6.7	5.2–8.2	5.1	3.7–6.4	9.4	6.4–12.4	7.2	4.8–9.6
1995	7.4	5.6–9.2	4.9	3.5–6.3	10.9	7.4–14.4	5.9	3.2–8.7
1998	8.3	6.3–10.2	4.4	3.0–5.7	11.4	8.6–14.2	5.2	2.7–7.7
2003	8	5.7–10.3	3.9	2.8–5.1	12.8	9.9–15.7	5.9	3.5–8.3
2010	7.8	5.8–9.8	3.4	2.6–4.2	10.4	7.7–13.1	3.7	2.2–5.1

Between 1993 and 2010, there was a decline in the average number of tree species seedlings per plot in the 2×2-m unfenced plots (Table 33). Seedling numbers in the fenced plots on Mount Misery and Mount Joy increased from 1993 to 1998, but declined in both locations in 2010. This is possibly due to increasing canopy closure and inhibiting low shade over the study years.

Table 33. Average number of tree species seedlings present per plot in the 2×2-m fenced and unfenced plots on Mount Misery and Mount Joy, Valley Forge National Historical Park, PA, 1993–2010.

Year	Mount Misery				Mount Joy			
	Fenced		Unfenced		Fenced		Unfenced	
	Mean	95% CI	Mean	95% CI	Mean	95% CI	Mean	95% CI
1993	17.7	8.4–27.0	11.8	3.9–19.7	6.5	2.0–10.9	3.7	1.1–6.2
1995	21.7	8.9–34.4	10.0	2.8–17.2	12.6	4.1–21.1	4.2	-2.1–10.5
1998	24.7	10.4–39.1	8.3	1.6–15.0	10.8	4.1–17.5	3.5	-1.4–8.8
2003	26	10.1–41.9	9.3	5.0–13.5	24.1	6.7–41.5	9.7	0.7–18.8
2010	17.5	8.2–26.9	3.8	1.8–5.8	8.9	3.9–14.0	1.0	0.1–1.9

The number of fenced and unfenced on plots on Mount Misery containing exotic species was low, but was highest in 1993 (mostly in fenced plots) and then declined through 2010 (Table 34). On Mount Joy, the number of fenced and unfenced plots containing exotic species was much higher than on Mount Misery for all survey years, with peak numbers in 2003. This was due to a large increase in exotics in the fenced plots during that year.

In 2003, five herbaceous species present at Valley Forge NHP were proposed as potential indicator species of the effects of deer browsing (Latham et al. 2005). These species are Jack-in-the-pulpit, wild sarsaparilla (*Aralia nudicaulis*), sweet cicely (*Osmorhiza claytoni*), Indian cucumber root (*Medeola virginiana*), and Trillium species (*Trillium* spp.). They occurred in six of 30 fenced plots (1–3 species present per plot), and one species (Jack-in-the-pulpit) was present in four of 30 unfenced plots in 2010 (Table 35). They occurred more frequently on Mount Joy than Mount Misery. Typically, when Jack-in-the-pulpit was present in an unfenced plot, it also occurred in the paired fenced plot (Table 35). There does not appear to be any trends through the years; a species occurrence in the initial year of survey (1993) in either a fenced or unfenced plot did not increase the chance that the species was found in later surveys. However, it does seem like species occurrences in any plot increased through 1995–2003, and then decreased slightly in the 2010 survey.

Table 34. Number of 2×2-m fenced and unfenced plots containing exotic species on Mount Misery and Mount Joy, Valley Forge National Historical Park, PA 1993–2010.

Area / Treatment	Scientific name	Common name	Plant type	1993	1995	1998	2003	2010
Mount Misery								
Fenced	*Polygonum caespitosum*	smartweed	herb	0	0	0	1	1
Fenced	*Prunus avium*	sweet cherry	tree	0	0	1	0	0
Fenced	*Lonicera japonica*	Japanese honeysuckle	vine	1	0	0	0	0
Fenced	*Polygonum aviculare*	knotweed	herb	1	0	1	0	0
Fenced	*Celastrus orbiculatus*	oriental bittersweet	vine	1	1	0	0	0
Fenced	*Microstegium vimineum*	stilt grass	herb	3	0	0	0	0
	Total species occurrences in fenced plots on Mount Misery			6	1	2	1	1
Unfenced	*Berberis thunbergii*	Japanese barberry	shrub	0	0	1	0	0
Unfenced	*Celastrus orbiculatus*	oriental bittersweek	vine	0	0	1	0	0
Unfenced	*Microstegium vimineum*	stilt grass	herb	1	1	0	0	0
	Total species occurrences in unfenced plots on Mount Misery			1	1	2	0	0
	Total species occurrences on Mount Misery			7	2	4	1	1
Mount Joy								
Fenced	*Ailanthus altissima*	tree of heaven	tree	0	0	0	2	0
Fenced	*Euonymus alata*	burnish bush	shrub	0	0	0	4	2
Fenced	*Lonicera morrowii*	honeysuckle	shrub	0	0	1	3	1
Fenced	*Polygonum aviculare*	knotweed	herb	0	0	3	0	0
Fenced	*Lonicera maackii*	amur honeysuckle	shrub	0	0	3	7	3
Fenced	*Paulownia tomentosa*	princess tree	tree	0	1	0	0	0
Fenced	*Rhodotypos scandens*	jetbead	shrub	0	1	1	1	1
Fenced	*Rosa multiflora*	multiflora rose	shrub	0	1	1	1	1
Fenced	*Acer platanoides*	Norway maple	tree	0	2	1	4	3
Fenced	*Berberis thunbergii*	Japanese barberry	shrub	1	0	0	0	0
Fenced	*Cardamine impatiens*	bitter-cress	herb	1	0	1	1	1
Fenced	*Purnus avium*	sweet cherry	tree	1	0	4	1	0
Fenced	*Ligustrum vulgare*	common privet	shrub	1	1	2	8	4
Fenced	*Duchesnea indica*	Indian strawberry	herb	2	0	1	0	1
Fenced	*Alliaria petiolata*	garlic-mustard	herb	2	0	6	7	4
Fenced	*Lonicera japonica*	Japanese honeysuckle	vine	2	7	4	5	4
Fenced	*Rubus phoenicolasius*	wineberry	shrub	3	2	2	6	3
Fenced	*Pastinaca sativa*	wild parsnip	herb	3	3	0	0	0
Fenced	*Celastrus orbiculatus*	oriental bittersweet	vine	5	5	8	7	4
Fenced	*Polygonum caespitosum*	smartweed	herb	6	3	0	2	0
Fenced	*Microstegium vimineum*	stilt grass	herb	6	3	2	5	2
Fenced	*Malva neglecta*	common mallow	herb	6	4	0	0	0
	Total species occurrences in fenced plots on Mount Joy			39	33	40	64	34
Unfenced	*Ligustrum vulgare*	common privet	shrub	0	0	0	1	0
Unfenced	*Ranunculus bulbosus*	bulbous buttercup	herb	0	0	0	1	0
Unfenced	*Taraxacum officinale*	common dandelion	herb	0	0	0	1	0
Unfenced	*Euonymus alata*	burning bush	shrub	0	0	0	2	1
Unfenced	*Lonicera maackii*	amur honeysuckle	shrub	0	0	0	3	0
Unfenced	*Acer platanoides*	Norway maple	tree	0	1	0	0	0
Unfenced	*Polygonum aviculare*	knotweed	herb	0	1	4	1	0
Unfenced	*Cardamine impatiens*	bitter-cress	herb	1	1	1	1	2
Unfenced	*Alliaria petiolata*	garlic-mustard	herb	1	1	5	3	1
Unfenced	*Prunus avium*	sweet cherry	tree	2	0	0	0	0
Unfenced	*Duchesnea indica*	Indian strawberry	herb	2	2	2	1	1
Unfenced	*Pastinaca sativa*	wild parsnip	herb	3	2	0	0	0
Unfenced	*Lonicera japonica*	Japanese honeysuckle	vine	3	4	2	2	0
Unfenced	*Microstegium vimineum*	stilt grass	herb	4	6	8	7	10
Unfenced	*Malva neglecta*	common mallow	herb	5	7	0	0	0
Unfenced	*Celastrus orbiculatus*	oriental bittersweet	vine	5	7	5	2	1
Unfenced	*Rubus phoenicolasius*	wineberry	shrub	6	2	2	2	0
Unfenced	*Polygonum caespitosum*	smartweed	herb	7	3	1	4	4
	Total species occurrences in unfenced plots on Mount Joy			39	37	30	31	20
	Total species occurrences on Mount Joy			78	70	70	95	54

Table 35. Occurrence (0 = absent; 1 = present) of Jack-in-the-pulpit (*Arisaema triphyllum*), wild sarsaparilla (*Aralia nudicaulis*), sweet cicely (*Osmorhiza claytoni*), Indian cucumber root (*Medeola virginiana*), and *Trillium* spp. in the 2×2-m fenced and unfenced plots on Mount Misery and Mount Joy, Valley Forge National Historical Park, PA 1993–2010.

Site Number	Treatment	Species	1993	1995	1998	2003	2010
Mount Misery							
7	Fenced	*Medeola virginiana*	1	1	1	0	0
7	Unfenced	*Medeola virginiana*	1	0	0	0	0
8	Fenced	*Aralia nudicaulis*	0	0	1	1	1
8	Unfenced	*Aralia nudicaulis*	0	0	0	0	0
9	Fenced	*Aralia nudicaulis*	0	0	1	0	0
9	Unfenced	*Aralia nudicaulis*	0	0	0	0	0
10	Fenced	*Medeola virginiana*	0	0	0	0	0
10	Unfenced	*Medeola virginiana*	1	0	1	0	0
11	Fenced	*Aralia nudicaulis*	1	0	1	1	1
11	Unfenced	*Aralia nudicaulis*	0	0	0	0	0
11	Fenced	*Arisaema triphyllum*	0	0	0	1	0
11	Unfenced	*Arisaema triphyllum*	0	0	0	1	0
11	Fenced	*Medeola virginiana*	0	1	1	1	1
11	Unfenced	*Medeola virginiana*	1	1	1	0	0
11	Fenced	*Trillium* spp.	0	1	0	0	0
11	Unfenced	*Trillium* spp.	1	0	0	0	0
Mount Joy							
16	Fenced	*Arisaema triphyllum*	0	1	1	1	0
16	Unfenced	*Arisaema triphyllum*	0	1	0	1	0
17	Fenced	*Arisaema triphyllum*	0	0	1	1	1
17	Unfenced	*Arisaema triphyllum*	0	0	1	1	1
17	Fenced	*Osmorhiza claytoni*	0	0	1	1	1
17	Unfenced	*Osmorhiza claytoni*	0	0	0	0	0
17	Fenced	*Trillium* spp.	1	0	0	0	0
17	Unfenced	*Trillium* spp.	1	0	0	0	0
19	Fenced	*Arisaema triphyllum*	0	0	0	1	1
19	Unfenced	*Arisaema triphyllum*	0	0	1	1	1
19	Fenced	*Osmorhiza claytoni*	0	0	1	0	0
19	Unfenced	*Osmorhiza claytoni*	0	0	0	0	0
21	Fenced	*Aralia nudicaulis*	0	0	1	0	0
21	Unfenced	*Aralia nudicaulis*	0	0	0	0	0
21	Fenced	*Osmorhiza claytoni*	1	1	0	0	1
21	Unfenced	*Osmorhiza claytoni*	0	0	0	0	0
24	Fenced	*Arisaema triphyllum*	0	0	0	1	0
24	Unfenced	*Arisaema triphyllum*	0	0	0	0	0
25	Fenced	*Arisaema triphyllum*	0	1	0	1	1
25	Unfenced	*Arisaema triphyllum*	0	1	0	1	1
25	Fenced	*Osmorhiza claytoni*	1	1	0	0	0
25	Unfenced	*Osmorhiza claytoni*	0	0	0	0	0
25	Fenced	*Trillium* spp.	1	0	0	0	0
25	Unfenced	*Trillium* spp.	0	0	0	0	0
27	Fenced	*Medeola virginiana*	0	0	0	0	0
27	Unfenced	*Medeola virginiana*	0	1	0	0	0
28	Fenced	*Arisaema triphyllum*	0	1	0	1	0
28	Unfenced	*Arisaema triphyllum*	0	1	1	1	1
28	Fenced	*Osmorhiza claytoni*	0	0	0	0	0
28	Unfenced	*Osmorhiza claytoni*	0	1	0	0	0
29	Fenced	*Arisaema triphyllum*	0	1	0	1	0
29	Unfenced	*Arisaema triphyllum*	0	1	0	0	0

Tree Seedling Stocking Rates

In 2010, 50% of the fenced plots at Mount Misery and Mount Joy were adequately stocked with all tree species combined (including exotics), whereas none of the unfenced plots were adequately stocked (Table 36). On Mount Misery, two-thirds of the 15 fenced plots were adequately stocked, whereas only one-third of the fenced plots on Mount Joy were adequately stocked. All of the stocked plots on Mount Joy were in the oak forest; none in the tuliptree forest. The stocking rate in the fenced plots has been increasing since 1993; a similar trend was not seen in the unfenced plots.

Table 36. Percent of adequately stocked fenced and unfenced plots, using all tree species data including exotics, on both Mount Misery and Mount Joy (n = 30 for each cell), Valley Forge National Historical Park, PA, 1993–2010.

Plot Type	1993	1995	1998	2003	2010
Fenced	3	3	13	27	50
Unfenced	3	0	0	0	0

The mean weighted tree seedling counts (in which seedling number is weighted by height) in the fenced plots are significantly higher than the unfenced plots in each year, despite the fact that the weighted value decreased from 2003 to 2010 (Table 37).

Table 37. Mean number of stems and standard error (weighted counts by height class for all tree species combined including exotics) per fenced and unfenced plot (4 m^2) on both Mount Misery and Mount Joy, Valley Forge National Historical Park, PA, 1993–2010.

Plot Type	1993		1995		1998		2003		2010	
	x	SE	x	SE	x	SE	x	SE	x	SE
Fenced	4.8	2.6	4.4	1.2	7.5	2.2	25.2	8.9	18.0	3.9
Unfenced	1.4	0.9	0.2	0.1	0.1	0.1	0.0		0.0	

Largay and Sneddon (2007) report on desired conditions of the future forest of Valley Forge National Historical Park. We have used Largay and Sneddon (2007) as a guideline for our management recommendations because of the importance of the desired species (mainly oak) for wildlife. However, they may not be chosen as final target conditions by the National Park Service. These conditions include two major desired forest types, the Dry Oak (a combination of Dry Oak and Dry-Mesic Chestnut Oak forests) and Mesophytic forests. The Dry Oak Forest will encompass the vast majority of the areas we have designated "Dry Oak" on both Mount Joy and Mount Misery; so, for the purposes of the analysis, we have combined the desired tree species for these two types and performed calculations on the full list of species (Table 38).

Table 38. Desired canopy and subcanopy tree species and tall and low shrub species of the Dry Oak (and Dry-Mesic Chestnut Oak) and Mesophytic desired forest types on Mount Joy and Mount Misery, Valley Forge National Historical Park, PA (Largay and Sneddon 2007).

Forest Type	Canopy	Subcanopy	Tall Shrub	Low Shrub
Dry Oak	chestnut oak black oak northern red oak tuliptree white oak scarlet oak American chestnut pignut hickory mockernut hickory shagbark hickory	red maple blackgum flowering dogwood	mountain laural mapleleaf viburnum witch hazel pink azalea	rarly lowbush blueberry black huckleberry wintergreen
Mesophytic	tuliptree northern red oak white oak black oak American beech American chestnut shagbark hickory mockernut hickory pignut hickory American basswood	red maple white ash American hornbeam flowering dogwood eastern redbud black walnut	mapleleaf viburnum northern spicebush	

The Largay and Sneddon (2007) report included stocking guidelines for the desired Dry Oak and Mesophytic forest types (Table 39). Fenced plots in the Dry Oak Forest are currently (2010) stocked for saplings and seedlings of all desired canopy and subcanopy tree species combined, as well as seedlings of desired oak species combined. The high numbers of current seedling stocking, for all species and for oaks, are due to the numbers of chestnut oak regeneration (~7,500 stems per ha). The remaining seedlings are mainly red maple and blackgum regeneration, which are desired subcanopy trees in this forest type; however, there are no oak saplings present throughout the 22 fenced plots contained within the Dry Oak Forest type. Even though red maple and blackgum are desired in the subcanopy, this does not mean that these species will not move into overstory dominance rather than stay in the subcanopy, especially if the other desired overstory species (i.e., oaks) are not present in the sapling layer. If oaks cannot succeed in recruiting to overstory dominance, it is likely that red maple and blackgum would fill the gap. The eight fenced plots in the Successional Tuliptree Forest (Mesophytic Forest desired condition) are not stocked for saplings or seedlings of all desired species combined. The fact that there are no oak saplings present in any fenced plots of either forest type highlights the bottleneck that occurs in recruitment of oak seedlings into the sapling layer. This is the main cause of regeneration failure in oak stands, and indicates that the desired Dry Oak Forest type may not be attainable without management designed to recruit oak saplings (see Discussion).

Table 39. Guidelines for stocking of desired species (per ha [from Largay and Sneddon 2007]) and current (species per ha [2010]) regeneration conditions in the 30 fenced plots (Dry Oak n=22, Mesophytic n=8) on Mount Joy and Mount Misery, Valley Forge National Historical Park, PA.

Desired Forest Type	Dry Oak			Mesophytic		
	Desired	Current	Stocked	Desired	Current	Stocked
Saplings (all spp.[1])	500	681.8	yes	3,000	625.0	no
Seedlings (all spp.)	5,400	30,454.5	yes	10,000	3,125.0	no
Saplings (oak[2])	10–100	0.0	no	none given	0.0	-
Seedlings (oak)	1,300–5,000	15,000.0	yes	none given	312.5	-

[1] all spp = all desired canopy and subcanopy tree species (in the Dry Oak Forest, all desired species from both the Dry Oak and Dry-Mesic Chestnut Oak variant forests are included).
[2] oak = all desired canopy and subcanopy oak species (in the Dry Oak Forest, all desired species from both the Dry Oak and Dry-Mesic Chestnut Oak variant forests are included).

The weighted number of seedlings of desired canopy tree species combined is significantly higher in the fenced plots in the Dry Oak versus Successional Tuliptree forest types, although the stocking rate in 2010 is inadequate in fenced plots of both types (based on McWilliams et al. 2002 criterion of 19,889 seedlings per ha; Table 40). The difference is due to the dominance of herbaceous and shrub species in the understory of the Successional Tuliptree Forest which is not unexpected, given the soil characteristics of this rich area as compared with the more xeric soils underlying the Dry Oak forests. Seedlings of most tree species will have difficulty competing for resources in fenced plots that are often crowded with exotic invasive species. The low regeneration numbers calculated with this method of determining stocking are due to the fact that the vast majority of regeneration is below 15 cm in height, which is given a weight of 0 (Table 2). The two ways of calculating density is the reason for the difference in Tables 39 and 40 when considering whether or not the stands were stocked or not stocked. The calculation involved in arriving at the values in Table 39 includes all seedlings, without assigning weights; therefore, also including the regeneration less than 15 cm in height, even though most of these individuals will likely not be competitive in the developing stand.

Table 40. Regeneration stocking rates for desired overstory species using weighted seedling per sapling counts per ha in 2010 in the 30 fenced plots (Dry Oak n=22, Mesophytic n=8) on Mount Joy and Mount Misery, Valley Forge National Historical Park, PA.

Forest Type	Species	Count/12.57 m^2	Count/ha
Dry Oak*	chestnut oak	9.6	7,613.6
	black oak	1.3	1,022.7
	northern red oak	0.7	568.2
	tuliptree	7.1	5,681.8
	white oak	0.0	0.0
	scarlet oak	0.0	0.0
	American chestnut	0.0	0.0
	pignut hickory	0.0	0.0
	mockernut hickory	0.0	0.0
	shagbark hickory	0.0	0.0
	Total	18.7	14886.4
Mesophytic	tuliptree	0.4	113.6
	northern red oak	0.0	0.0
	white oak	0.0	0.0
	black oak	0.0	0.0
	American beech	0.0	0.0
	American chestnut	0.0	0.0
	shagbark hickory	0.0	0.0
	mockernut hickory	0.0	0.0
	pignut hickory	0.0	0.0
	American basswood	0.0	0.0
	Total	0.4	113.6

* Included desired species of Dry Oak and Dry-Mesic Chestnut Oak Forest Types.

Discussion

We are *not* confident that the existing overstory oak and hickory at Valley Forge NHP will be replaced by new trees of the desired species (Largay and Sneddon 2007) at a sufficient rate over the next century or more, despite the scarcity of red maple and the substantial number of chestnut oak seedlings on the drier shale sites on Mount Misery. Current conditions in the Dry Oak forests meet desired tree species composition in the canopy and subcanopy; however, the understory conditions, due to deep shade and heavy deer browse, are not conducive to the next generation of desirable tree species. While tree mortality is a frequent occurrence in the region due to wind-throw, ice storm damage, gypsy moth defoliation, and drought, most disturbances form single tree canopy gaps that are typically too small to provide adequate light to promote successful oak recruitment into the forest canopy (Berg 2004, Jacobs et al. 2006, Collins and Battaglia 2008). Desirable subcanopy species (such as red maple, blackgum, flowering dogwood, white ash, and redbud), while present, can inhibit oak and hickory from successfully reaching the canopy. They mainly exist due to their high shade tolerance. Oak and hickory must first be established and successfully regenerate before these subcanopy species can be promoted. It is our opinion that the three forests used in this study are in need of long-term management techniques that have been applied throughout eastern oak forests (Brose and Van Lear 1998, Brose et al. 2008, Steiner et al. 2008, Abrams and Sands 2010). These techniques include the following:

- Thinning from below of trees other than oak and hickory to increase available light for understory oak and hickory and to eliminate low shade that favors shade-tolerant species such as red maple, sugar maple, striped maple (*A. pensylvanicum*), and witch-hazel.

- Crown thinning of trees other than oak and hickory to create larger canopy openings, eliminate seed sources of competing tree species, and to increase available light for existing seedlings, saplings, and future mast production.

- The use of periodic low- to moderate-intensity understory fire to eliminate undesirable species, create oak and hickory seedling sprouts with an enhanced growth rate, and create favorable germination conditions for new seedlings. Although this is not currently a management option at Valley Forge NHP, it is the preferred approach and could possibly be implemented in the future. However, if the preferred approach cannot be implemented, understory thinning and use of herbicides may be used to simulate the outcome of prescribed burning. Several successive burns or thinning/herbicide applications may be needed during early stand development to stimulate oak and hickory seedling growth and then again in the middle and late stages to eliminate undesirable species.

- Properly timed and appropriate application of herbicide to stems and cut stumps of undesirable hardwoods to prevent sprouting and root suckering.

- Weeding of undesirable seedlings and saplings.

- Maintaining relatively low deer populations throughout the park.

These management actions and others (such as planting oak and hickory seedlings) will be discussed for each of the three stands at Valley Forge NHP. The recommended actions should promote the recruitment of new oak and hickory trees over the next several decades and prevent the "natural" succession to shade-tolerant red maple and blackgum (and other trees) that is occurring in the study area. In addition, this Discussion section will include:

- the monitoring protocol and timing for future data collection;

- management prescriptions to close the gap between existing and desired forest conditions (based on Largay and Sneddon [2007]);

- minimum management prescriptions and deer density considered necessary to promote tree regenerations regardless of species composition; and

- successional trajectory in the absence of active forest management. Forest management prescriptions will assume a deer density of 31–35 deer per forested sq mi.

Largay and Sneddon (2007) described tuliptree forests at Valley Forge NHP, such as the one we surveyed on Mount Joy, as Successional Tuliptree Forest: Mesophytic Forest (on slightly alkaline soils). They believe that this early successional community occurs in areas that were previously cleared or created by fill and that some of the stands at Valley Forge NHP were planted. In our opinion, the Successional Tuliptree Forest on Mount Joy formed following agricultural abandonment or old-field succession in the early 1900's (Rhoads et al. 1989). Largay and Sneddon (2007) concluded that the Successional Tuliptree Forest is an undesirable type because it has no known natural or historical analog. They propose that the desired condition of this type of forest is the conversion to a native Mesophytic Forest type (white oak) with high ecological integrity. We don't necessarily agree that a tuliptree forest is an undesirable type or that it lacks natural or historical analogs. Indeed, tuliptree forests commonly exist in cove (sideslope ravines) ecosystems throughout the central and southern Appalachian Mountains and it persists in mesophytic oak and hardwood forests due to its ability to seed into and capture canopy gaps. Tuliptree is intolerant of shade (thus early successional), but often occurs as a gap-phase species; the latter explains its presence in middle- to late-successional forests (Burns and Honkala 1990). Nonetheless, the Successional Tuliptree Forest we studied on the lower slope of Mount Joy is an anthropogenic artifact of past clearing, farming, and/or grazing, and should be managed with the desired Mesophytic Forest type species composition in mind.

The tuliptree stand on Mount Joy (with 50% overstory relative importance) has a small oak overstory component (about 10% relative importance value) and a very sparse woody understory (Figure 6). Hickory species are very underrepresented, making up only about five percent of the relative importance value (Table 4), compared with about 15% in the pre-settlement forest (Mikan et al. 1994). The understory has minimal shrub cover and is almost totally dominated by Japanese stiltgrass (72% cover; Table 8), which deer avoid due to its reputed toxicity. The few tree seedlings that do exist (3,000 per ha; Table 6) in the forest are all in the smallest height category (5–15 cm) and grow in a suppressed state within the stiltgrass canopy, with very few oak or hickory seedlings. Desirable subcanopy species occur in low densities outside the fenced exclosures (sapling numbers of red maple, redbud, white ash, and flowering dogwood, combined, are 100.3 per ha; Table 5). Moreover, not all desirable subcanopy species are present, including black walnut (*Juglans nigra*) and American hornbeam (*Carpinus caroliniana*). The deer exclosures have a much larger number and height for tree seedlings and shrub species than the unfenced plots, but they have a scarcity of oak seedlings (only 15% of the total number of seedlings) and saplings. The oak seedlings are also small compared to the height of co-occurring red maple, slippery elm, black cherry, and blackgum seedlings growing within the exclosures, which is expected, based on the species' growth rates. Without disturbance or active management, this will make it difficult for the over-topped oak seedlings to grow into saplings and beyond.

There is a total lack of hickory seedlings and saplings in both fenced and unfenced plots in the tuliptree stand on Mount Joy; therefore, we conclude that reducing deer populations to 31–35 per forested sq mi within the tuliptree forests is a necessary initial step. However, our data suggest that additional management activities are required to promote adequate oak and hickory regeneration and recruitment into the overstory and to facilitate desirable subcanopy species. However, it is important to realize that a subcanopy dominated by tree species other than oak and hickory will likely interfere with future oak and hickory recruitment into the canopy. This will be exacerbated by the fact that many of the desirable subcanopy trees are more shade tolerant (e.g., red maple and dogwood), whereas oak and hickory are light demanding.

The successional trajectory of the Successional Tuliptree Forest in the absence of active management (including deer populations >35 per forested sq mi) is the continuation of tuliptree dominance in the overstory and stiltgrass dominance in the understory for the next 100 years or more, with little overstory or subcanopy recruitment for any tree species, and minimal shrub cover. If deer populations are reduced to 31–35 per forested sq mi, recruitment of the shade-tolerant red maple, Norway maple, slippery elm, and blackgum trees into the overstory is likely. Some, but not all, of these are desirable species for the subcanopy. However, Horsley et al. (2003) reported data that indicate deer population levels above 21 per forested sq mi (8 per km^2) in northern hardwood forests is problematic to favored browse species. We assume this would apply to oak and hickory at Valley Forge NHP. The cutting of a significant number of tuliptrees from the forest overstory to increase subcanopy and understory light levels and the active management of exotic plant species for several years following canopy openings (including a large reduction in Japanese stiltgrass cover) will be required to increase oak and hickory regeneration and recruitment.

According to Largay and Sneddon (2007), the target vegetation structure and composition for the Successional Tuliptree: Mesophytic Forest consists of a mixed canopy of white oak, black oak, northern red oak, American beech, tuliptree, shagbark hickory (*C. ovata*), mockernut hickory (*C. alba* or *C. tomentosa*), and pignut hickory (*C. glabra*), with red maple, white ash, American hornbeam, flowering dogwood, redbud, and black walnut in the subcanopy. In terms of the management of this forest to promote its conversion to a forest of the recommended species composition, we recommend the following:

- Cutting 75–90% of the existing tuliptrees and other *non-target* tree species (in late summer) from the stand, leaving the remaining trees as scattered individuals. A systemic herbicide (such as glyphosate) should be applied within 24 hours after tree felling to the cut stumps of trees under 30 in dbh to prevent stump sprouting. Tree stumps larger than 30 in dbh (mostly tuliptree) will probably not be capable of producing stump sprouts.

Opening the canopy in this way may encourage reproduction of some shrub species, particularly nonnative invasives that will have to be controlled with additional herbicide applications.

- Cutting and applying stump herbicide to most of the red maple and all of the Norway maple, sweet cherry (*P. avium*), and black locust trees in the stand. We recommend leaving about 50 red maple trees per ha (about 20 per ac) as seed trees to produce the desired subcanopy red maple. It is critically important to apply herbicide to the stumps of black locust because of its ability to produce a large number of root suckers throughout the forest.

- Applying herbicide to all or most of the stiltgrass understory as well as any nonnative shrubs. Indeed, these species may be promoted by the removal of overstory trees. If this action is not taken, we anticipate that the stiltgrass and nonnative shrubs will interfere (via normal competition or allelopathy) with the regeneration and recruitment of the desired tree species. Native shrub species (such as witch hazel) may also increase following overstory removal and should be monitored and controlled by physical removal or herbicides if they interfere with regeneration and recruitment of desired species.

- Planting approximately 750 seedlings per ha (300 per ac) in planting tubes throughout the forest in the following proportion:

Target Species Composition (from Largay and Sneddon 2007)

Species	Target Cover Range
White oak	10–25%
Black oak	10–25%
Northern red oak	10–25%
American beech	10–25%
Shagbark hickory	5–10%
Mockernut hickory	5–10%
Pignut hickory	5–10%

- Tree species desired in the subcanopy, such as red maple and blackgum, are presently regenerating in the Successional Tuliptree forest type; therefore, no planting of these species is required at this time. However, other subcanpoy species not present in sufficient numbers (e.g., black walnut and American hornbeam) will need to be planted at about 740 seedlings per ha (300 seedlings per ac).

The Dry Oak Forest surveyed on Mount Joy for this project has a moderately high oak overstory component (about 40% relative importance value across five oak species). In terms of individual species, the stand is dominated by blackgum (15.8% relative importance value) and red maple (12.4% relative importance value), as well as tuliptree (9.7% relative importance value). Very few oak saplings and seedlings exist in the forest compared with moderately high numbers that exist for blackgum, red maple, and sassafras. Current canopy (oak-dominated) and subcanopy (red maple and blackgum dominated) tree composition contain an adequate number of desirable species; however, we do not believe that this condition will persist through the next generation (about 100 years from now). Shrub cover is presently low throughout? the unfenced portions of the forest, while Japanese stiltgrass represents 10% cover for the herbaceous species. The fenced exclosures within the forest have a much larger number and height of tree seedlings and shrub species than the unfenced plots, but few saplings. In the fenced plots, seedlings total 36,429 per ha and are dominated by red maple, white ash, and blackgum (totaling 27,857 seedlings per ha), two of which (red maple and blackgum) are desirable in the subcanopy (Table 22). In contrast, oaks total only 1,786 per ha (<5%) of the seedling population in the fenced plots. Hickory seedlings (and saplings) are nonexistent in both fenced and unfenced plots. Total shrub cover is 35% in the fenced plots compared with only 3% in the unfenced plots (Table 23).

We conclude that reducing deer populations to 31–35 per forested sq mi within the Dry Oak Forest on Mount Joy will help towards producing an adequate number of oak and hickory seedlings, but this likelihood would be greater if deer density was brought down to about 20 per forested sq mi (cf. Horsley et al. 2003). The recruitment of new oak and hickory seedlings into the overstory will also require additional management actions (see below). This is due to the low to moderate shade tolerance of eastern oak species (Abrams 1992). The successional trajectory of this forest in the absence of active management (including high deer populations >35 per forested sq mi) is the continuation of mixed-oak dominance in the overstory for the next 100 years or more, coupled with minimal overstory recruitment for red maple and blackgum, and no recruitment for other tree species (especially oak and hickory). If deer populations are reduced to 31 to 35 per forested sq mi, increased recruitment of red maple and blackgum trees into the overstory is likely to occur with natural successional trajectories (replacing early successional tuliptree and mid-successional oak species), which is not a desirable condition according to Largay and Sneddon (2007). These species are desired in the subcanopy, but not the canopy, of the Dry Oak Forest.

According to Largay and Sneddon (2007), the target vegetation structure and composition for the Dry Oak Forest canopy dominants include chestnut oak, black oak, and American chestnut, with less frequent white oak, scarlet oak, and northern red oak. Scattered tuliptree may also be present in the canopy. Red maple, blackgum, and flowering dogwood are typical subcanopy trees. Current overstory and subcanopy dominants partially meet the desired conditions; however inhibiting factors in the understory will prevent the continuation of desired species dominance and the necessary increase in hickory over the coming decades. In terms of the management of this forest to promote its conversion to a forest of the recommended species composition, we recommend the following:

- cutting 75% of the existing *non-target* trees (in late summer) from the stand, leaving the remaining trees as scattered individuals. A systemic herbicide (such as glyphosate) should be applied within 24 hours after tree felling to the cut stumps of the non-target trees under 30 in dbh to prevent stump sprouting. Understory composition should be monitored following overstory cutting; if exotic invasive species such as stiltgrass increase in density and inhibit desired regeneration, cutting and herbicide treatments should be implemented.

- planting approximately 300 seedlings per ha in planting tubes throughout the forest in the following proportion. The planted seedlings, coupled with the expected increase in natural regeneration of oaks following overstory removal, should result in adequate sapling and overstory recruitment over the next few decades, pending an ample reduction in deer density.

Target Species Composition (from Largay and Sneddon 2007)

Species	Target Canopy Cover
Chestnut oak	20–40%
Black oak	10–40%
Scarlet oak	5–15%
White oak	5–10%
Northern red oak	5–10%
Tuliptree	5%

- Tree species desired in the subcanopy (red maple, blackgum, and flowering dogwood) are present in adequate numbers in the Dry Oak Forest stand on Mount Joy; therefore, no planting is recommended at this time. However, if these species are not able to regenerate successfully following the planting and establishment of the desired overstory trees, plantings may become necessary.

The Dry Oak Forest on Mount Misery has a moderately high oak overstory component (about 51% relative importance value across five oak species). Other dominant tree species in the stand include blackgum (14.5 % relative importance value), red maple (13.9 % relative importance value), and tuliptree (10.4 % relative importance value) (Table 14). Very few oak saplings and seedlings exist in the unfenced areas of the forest relative to that for blackgum, red maple, and sassafras. Desirable subcanopy species (red maple, blackgum, and flowering dogwood) are well represented. Shrub and herb cover is low throughout the unfenced portions of the forest. However, tall thickets of mountain laurel exist in certain areas, which is a desirable condition in this forest type, provided it does not interfere with tree species regeneration. The fenced exclosures within the forest have a much greater number and height for tree seedlings and shrub species than the unfenced plots, but few saplings. In the fenced plots, tree seedlings total 43,833 per ha and are dominated by chestnut oak, sassafras, red maple, and blackgum (Table 25). They are unique because of the high density of chestnut oak seedlings (19,833 per ha). In contrast, oak seedlings total only 1,833 per ha in the unfenced plots. Hickory seedlings are also scarce in both fenced and unfenced plots. Total shrub cover is 24% in the fenced plots compared with only 2% in the unfenced plots (Table 26). We conclude that reducing deer populations to 31–35 per forested sq mi within the Dry Oak Forest stand on Mount Misery may promote some additional oak regeneration, but probably not the full complement that would be possible if deer populations were reduced to about 20 per forested sq mi. In addition, forest cutting to increase light levels in the understory and subcanopy is needed to promote adequate oak height growth into sapling and overstory height classes.

The successional trajectory of this forest in the absence of active management (including high deer populations >35 per forested sq mi) is the continuation of mixed-oak dominance in the overstory for the next 100 years or more, coupled with increased overstory recruitment for red maple and blackgum. If deer populations are reduced to fewer than 35 per forested sq mi, recruitment of red maple and blackgum trees into the overstory is likely to increase unless they are removed during forest management procedures. In this case, these desirable subcanopy species would be allowed to seed back in following successful oak regeneration and height growth, along with flowering dogwood.

According to Largay and Sneddon (2007), the target vegetation structure and composition for the Dry Oak Forest canopy dominants include chestnut oak, black oak, and American chestnut with less frequent white oak, scarlet oak, and northern red oak. Scattered tuliptree may also be present in the canopy. Red maple, blackgum, and flowering dogwood are typical subcanopy trees. In terms of the management of this forest to promote its conversion to a forest of the recommended species composition, we recommend the following prescriptions, which are similar to that of the Dry Oak Forest on Mount Joy. However, the oak forest on Mount Misery presently contains an adequate number of chestnut oak seedlings and therefore additional seedlings for this species do not have to be planted:

- Cutting 75% of the existing *non-target* trees (in late summer) from the stand, leaving the remaining trees as scattered individuals. A systemic herbicide (such as glyphosate) should be applied within 24 hours after tree felling to the cut stumps of the trees under 30 in dbh to prevent stump sprouting. Mountain laurel cover should be monitored with overstory removal; if it is seen to be inhibiting regeneration, cutting and stump herbicide treatment should be implemented.

- Planting approximately 300 seedlings per ha in planting tubes throughout the forest in the following proportion. The planted seedling, coupled with the expected increase in natural regeneration of oaks following overstory removal, should result in adequate sapling and overstory recruitment pending an ample reduction in deer density.

  Target Species Composition (from Largay and Sneddon 2007)

Species	Target Canopy Cover
Black oak	20–40%
Scarlet oak	15–20%
White oak	15–20%
Northern red oak	10–20%
Tuliptree	5–10%

- Two of the tree species desired in the subcanopy (red maple and blackgum) are present in the Dry Oak Forest stand on Mount Misery, therefore no planting is recommended at this time. Flowering dogwood, desired in 5–20% of the forest subcanopy, is not sufficiently present at this time; therefore, we recommend that the natural regeneration following cutting be monitored and flowering dogwood be planted if necessary.

Our recommended monitoring protocol for future data collection is the same methodology used for this study and described in detail in our Methods section. This includes sampling the sixty 20×20-m overstory and understory plots and the 30 paired 2×2-m fenced and unfenced plots, using a single 2×2-m plot for fenced and unfenced understory plots (as opposed to four 1-m^2

subplots as used in 2003). The future timing for resurveying all the unfenced plots involved in this study (both the 2×2-m and 20×20-m plots) should be fairly short intervals to capture the potentially rapid vegetation changes we expect to occur in response the reduction in deer populations and future recommended forest cutting and herbicide application. We recommend that all the unfenced plots be surveyed at two-year intervals over the next 10 years. However, the overstory component of the 20×20-m plots does not have to be surveyed until after the forest cutting of non-target trees has occurred. We recommend that the 2×2-m fenced plots be surveyed at five-year intervals. This will allow for a vegetation comparison of plots with no deer browsing versus those with reduced deer browsing (e.g., the unfenced plots following a reduction in deer density).

Conclusion

In our opinion, the Successional Tuliptree Forest on Mount Joy formed after agricultural abandonment during the last century (Rhoads et al. 1993). While being dominated by overstory tuliptree, it contains a fairly diverse mixture of other tree species, including oaks, in the forest canopy and subcanopy. In contrast, Japanese stiltgrass overwhelmingly dominated (72% cover) the forest understory (Table 8); this is likely the result of intensive deer browsing of other woody and herbaceous plant species. In the Dry Oak Forest on Mount Joy and Mount Misery, scarlet oak, black oak, chestnut oak, red oak, and white oak share overstory dominance. We believe these stands have always been forested, despite past tree harvesting, and were not totally cleared and used for agriculture as was the area that is now Successional Tuliptree Forest. Fire suppression and deer browsing have resulted in low to moderate sapling and seedling densities in all three stands and these regeneration classes were primarily dominated by shade-tolerant red maple, blackgum, and sassafras. Numbers of oak seedlings and saplings were particularly low to nonexistent in all three stands, with the exception of chestnut oak seedlings (875 per ha recorded in unfenced 20×20-m plots) on Mount Misery. The management prescriptions outlined in this report are required to produce the next generation of desired oak and hickory species. If no actions are taken, a change to more shade-tolerant tree species will occur as a result of normal forest succession that takes place in eastern oak forests in the absence of periodic burning.

In terms of the fenced and unfenced plots, we recorded low densities of seedlings and saplings, especially for oak and hickory species, in the unfenced plots. In contrast, the fenced plots contained 33,133 seedlings per ha and were dominated by chestnut oak, followed by red maple, sassafras, blackgum, and white ash. The Successional Tuliptree Forest on Mount Joy contained lower seedling density and fewer oak seedlings than the Dry Oak Forest stands, due mostly to very high stiltgrass cover in unfenced areas. Very few saplings of any tree species were recorded in the 18-year old fenced plots and none of them were oak or hickory. In many cases, fenced plots, especially in the Successional Tuliptree forest, were dominated by exotic shrub and herbaceous species. Weconclude that regeneration stocking of desired tree species is inadequate even in the fenced plots because of the suppressed growth of the existing seedlings and high level of competing vegetation. The proposed composition of the desired forest types is currently met in the Dry Oak Forests on Mount Joy and Mount Misery. However regeneration (of oak and hickory) is not sufficient to perpetuate these conditions over the longer-term. Canopy conditions in the Successional Tuliptree Forest do not currently meet desired conditions, although subcanopy conditions are partially adequate. Forest management recommendations proposed here should foster increased target species regeneration and recruitment across both forest types. Our recommendations include the harvesting of non-target trees, herbicide application to cut stumps, Japanese stiltgrass, and other inhibiting exotic species, and planting seedlings of targeted tree species, focusing mainly on restoring oak and hickory regeneration in the forest understory.

References Cited

Abrams, M. D. 1992. Fire and the development of oak forests. Bioscience 42:346–353.

Abrams, M. D. 1998. The red maple paradox. BioScience 48:355–364.

Abrams, M. D. 2002. The postglacial history of oak forests in eastern North America. *In:* Oaks Forest ecosystems, edited by W. J. McShea and W. M. Healy. Pages 34–45. The John Hopkins University Press.

Abrams, M. D. 2003. Where has all the white oak gone? BioScience 53:927–939.

Abrams, M. D., and B. A. Sands. 2010. Oak forest composition on contrasting soil types at the Mohonk Preserve, eastern New York. Northern Journal of Applied Forestry 27:105–109.

Abrams, M. D., and G. J. Nowacki. 1992. Historical variation in fire, oak recruitment, and post-logging accelerated succession in Pennsylvania. Bulletin of the Torrey Botanical Club 119:19–28.

Abrams, M. D., and G. J. Nowacki. 2008. Native Americans as active and passive promoters of mast and fruit trees in the eastern USA. The Holocene 18:1123–1137.

Berg, E. C. 2004. Upland oak ecology symposium: history, current conditions, and sustainability. *In:* Spetich, M. A., editor, General Technical Report SRS–73. Asheville, NC: U.S. Department of Agriculture, Forest Service, Southern Research Station. Pages 143–149.

Brose, P. H., and D. H. Van Lear. 1998. Responses of hardwood advance regeneration to seasonal prescribed fires in oak-dominated shelterwood stands. Canadian Journal of Forest Research. 28:331–339.

Brose, P. H., K. W. Gottschalk, S. B. Horsley, P. D. Knopp, J. N. Kochenderfer, B. J. McGuinness, G. W. Miller, T. E. Ristau, S. H. Stoleson, and S. L. Stout. 2008. Prescribing regeneration treatments for mixed-oak forests in the Mid-Atlantic region. General Technical Report NRS-33. Newtown Square, PA: U.S. Department of Agriculture, Forest Service, Northern Research Station. 100 pp.

Burns, R. M., and B. H. Honkala. 1990. Silvics of North America, vol. 2: Hardwoods. Washington (DC): US Department of Agriculture. Agricultural Handbook 654.

Collins, B., and L. Battaglia. 2008. Oak regeneration in southeastern bottomland hardwood forest. Forest Ecology and Management 255: 3026–3034.

Comiskey, J. A., J. P. Schmit, and G. Tierney. 2009. Mid-Atlantic Network forest vegetation monitoring protocol. Natural Resource Report NPS/MIDN/NRR—2009/119 National Park Service, Fort Collins, CO.

Delcourt, H. R., and P.A. Delcourt. 1997. Pre-Columbian Native American use of fire on the southern Appalachian landscape. Conservation Biology 11:1010–14.

Diefenbach, D. R., W. C. Vreeland, and K. M. Heister. 2008. Statistical analysis of understory vegetation data from Valley Forge National Historical Park, Pennsylvania, 1993–2003. Technical Report NPS/NER/NRTR—2008/118.

Ducey, M. J., W. K. Moser, and M. S. Ashton. 1996. Effect of fire intensity on under-story composition and diversity in a *Kalmia*-dominated oak forest, New England, USA. Vegetation 123:81–90.

Fei, S., and K. C. Steiner. 2007. Evidence for increasing red maple abundance in the eastern United States. Forest Science 53:473–477.

Fei, S., and K. C. Steiner. 2009. Rapid capture of growing space by red maple. Canadian Journal of Forest Research 39:1444–1452.

Horsley, S. B., S. L. Stout, and D. S. DeCalesta. 2003. White-tailed deer impact on the vegetation dynamics of a northern hardwood forest. Ecological Applications 13:98–118.

Jacobs, D. F., R. A. Rathfon, A. S. Davis, and D. E. Carlson. 2006. Stocktype and harvest gap size influence northern red oak regeneration success. 2006. Connor, Kristina F., editor, Proceedings of the 13th biennial southern silvicultural research conference. General Technical Report SRS–92. Asheville, NC: U.S. Department of Agriculture, Forest Service, Southern Research Station. Pp. 247–250.

Kittredge, D. B., and P. M. S. Ashton. 1990. Natural regeneration patterns in even-aged mixed stands in southern New England. Northern Journal of Applied Forestry 7:163–168.

Largay, E., and L. A. Sneddon. 2007. An approach to quantifying desired forest conditions at Valley Forge National Historical Park. Technical Report NPS/NER/NRTR—2007/082.

Latham, R. E., J. Beyea, M. Benner, C. A. Dunn, M. A. Fajvan, R. R. Freed, M. Grund, S. B. Horsley, A. F. Rhoads, and B. P. Shissler. 2005. Managing White-tailed Deer in Forest Habitat from an Ecosystem Perspective: Pennsylvania Case Study. Report by the Deer Management Forum for Audubon Pennsylvania and Pennsylvania Habitat Alliance, Harrisburg. URL: http://pa.audubon.org/deer_report.html#exec.

Lorimer, C. G. 1985. The role of fire in the perpetuation of oak forests. *In:* Challenges in Oak Management and Utilization (J. E. Johnson, editor). Cooperative Extension Service, University of Wisconsin, Madison, WI. Pp. 8–25.

Lorimer, C. G., and A. S. White. 2003. Scale and frequency of natural disturbances in the northeastern United States: implications for early successional forest habitat and regional age distributions. Forest Ecology and Management 185:41–64.

McGee, G. G, D. J. Leopold, and R. D. Nyland. 1995. Understory response to springtime prescribed fire in two New York transition oak forests. Forest Ecology and Management 76:149–168.

McWilliams, W. H., R. A. O'Brien, G. C. Reese, and K. L. Waddell. 2002. Distribution and abundance of oaks in North America. In: McShea, W. J. and W. H. Healy, editors, Oak forest ecosystems: ecology and management for wildlife. Baltimore, MD: Johns Hopkins Press: 13–32.

Miken, C. J., D. A. Orwig, and M. D. Abrams. 1994. Age structure and successional dynamics of a presettlement-origin chestnut oak forest in the Pennsylvania Piedmont. Bulletin of the Torrey Botanical Club 121:13–23.

Moser, W. K., M. J. Ducey, and P. M. S. Ashton. 1996. Effects of fire intensity on competitive dynamics between red and black oaks and mountain laurel. Northern Journal of Applied Forestry 13:119–123.

Nowacki, G. J., and M. D. Abrams. 2008. Demise of fire and mesophication of eastern U.S. forests. BioScience 58:123–138.

Podniesinski, G. S., L. A. Sneddon, J. Lundgren, H. Devine, B. Slocumb, and F. Koch. 2005. Vegetation classification and mapping of Valley Forge National Historical Park. Technical Report NPS/NER/NRTR—2005/028. National Park Service. Philadelphia, PA.

Rhoads, A. F., and W. M. Klein, Jr. 1993. The Vascular Flora of Pennsylvania: Annotated Checklist and Atlas. American Philosophical Society, Philadelphia, PA. 636 pp.

Rhoads, A. F., D. Ryan, and E. W. Aderman. 1989. Land use study of Valley Forge National Historical Park. Final Report, NPS. 225 pp.

Schuster, W. S. F., K. L. Griffin, et al. 2008. Changes in composition, structure and aboveground biomass over seventy-six years (1930–2006) in the Black Rock Forest, Hudson Highlands, southeastern New York State. Tree Physiology 28:537–549.

Steiner, K. C., J. C. Finley, P. J. Gould, S. Fei, and M. McDill. 2008. Oak regeneration guidelines for the central Appalachians. Northern Journal of Applied Forestry 25:5–16.

Whitney, G. G. 1994. From Coastal Wilderness to Fruited Plain. Cambridge University Press, Cambridge, U.K. 451 pp.

Appendix A. Plot locational information (northing and easting given in UTM Zone 18N) for the sixty 20×20-m plots established in spring 2010 on Mount Joy and Mount Misery (20 each in three forest stands: Mount Joy Successional Tuliptree, Mount Joy Dry Oak, and Mount Misery Dry Oak).

Site	Forest Type	Plot ID	Northing	Easting
Mount Joy	Dry Oak	J_02colocated_22uf	461415.4849	4439130.4604
		J_05_new	461294.3239	4438978.0062
		J_06_new	460759.7932	4438787.7235
		J_09_new	460856.7540	4438693.5642
		J_10_new	460755.6790	4438643.0187
		J_11_new	460834.3112	4438602.1886
		J_12_new	460974.1618	4438634.7374
		J_13_new	461034.1771	4438613.7191
		J_14_new	461294.9611	4438460.4661
		J_15_colocated_26uf	461235.8839	4438388.7118
		J_17_new	461309.5815	4438323.5362
		J_19_colocated_27uf	461219.5410	4438212.2137
		J_20_new	461305.6581	4438148.3521
		J_21_new	461423.2370	4438196.7454
		J_22_colocated_20uf	461499.5422	4438220.8443
		J_24_new	461603.6959	4438155.3961
		J_27_new	461544.1694	4438168.2480
		J_28_new	461367.2832	4438085.9826
		J_29_new	461293.1671	4438043.1744
		J_30_new	461270.0735	4437885.1138
	Successional Tuliptree	T_01_new	461597.2023	4438969.7585
		T_03_colocated_17uf	461527.7781	4438948.4330
		T_06_new	461461.9767	4438514.0032
		T_07_colocated_25uf	461447.9926	4438402.6559
		T_09_new	461572.6636	4438270.9730
		T_10_new	461688.2092	4438170.7200
		T_11_new	461681.4301	4438090.5201
		T_12_new	461620.4325	4438001.9712
		T_13_new	461595.0029	4437983.7902
		T_14_new	461459.3397	4437687.2960
		T_15_colocated_19uf	461381.0492	4437644.7213
		T_17_new	461263.1162	4437733.0268
		T_20_colocated_21uf	461342.1012	4437817.9093
		T_22_new	461466.6710	4437933.3744
		T_23_new	461235.7186	4438571.6566
		T_26_new	461137.7525	4438717.5079
		T_27_new	460959.5244	4438710.2731
		T_28_colocated_16uf	460954.9886	4438838.0347
		T_30_new	460845.8574	4438878.8822
		T_31_new	460949.8793	4438788.0452
Mount Misery	Dry Oak	M_01_new	460087.1822	4437351.2598
		M_03_colocated_01uf	460145.3112	4437489.1480
		M_04_colocated_02uf	460237.6430	4437328.0573
		M_06_colocated_03uf	460397.4795	4437491.0006
		M_09_colocated_04uf	460452.1745	4437580.1221
		M_10_new	460514.3836	4437494.4280
		M_12_colocated_05uf	460731.9769	4437655.4109
		M_14_colocated_06uf	460791.4330	4437717.2994
		M_16_new	460887.7218	4437746.4902
		M_19_new	460764.8893	4437853.1475
		M_21_colocated_08uf	460678.1965	4337947.8228
		M_22_new	460796.9897	4438022.2597
		M_25_new	460649.7431	4438198.4120
		M_26_new	460760.1212	4438196.6679
		M_27_new	460525.5879	4438211.0492
		M_32_new	460326.1563	4438123.4366
		M_33_colocated_12uf	460258.8513	4438166.5945
		M_35_colocated_13uf	460367.2561	4438250.5781
		M_37_colocated_14uf	460350.5101	4438322.0980
		M_39_new	460436.1108	4438590.8965

Appendix B. Species list for all plots (20×20-m plots and 2×2-m paired fenced and unfenced plots).

Vegetation Type Plot	Scientific name	Common name
Mount Joy Successional Tuliptree		
Tree	Acer platanoides	Norway maple
	Acer rubrum	red maple
	Acer saccharum	sugar maple
	Ailanthus altissima	tree of heaven
	Carya cordiformis	bitternut hickory
	Carya glabra	pignut hickory
	Carya tomentosa	mockernut hickory
	Celtis occidentalis	common hackberry
	Cercis Canadensis	redbud
	Cornus florida	flowering dogwood
	Fraxinus americana	white ash
	Liriodendron tulipifera	tuliptree
	Nyssa sylvatica	blackgum
	Pinus strobus	white pine
	Prunus avium	sweet cherry
	Prunus serotina	black cherry
	Prunus virginiana	choke cherry
	Quercus alba	white oak
	Quercus coccinea	scarlet oak
	Quercus montana	chestnut oak
	Quercus rubra	red oak
	Quercus velutina	black oak
	Robinia pseudoacacia	black locust
	Sassafras albidum	sassafras
Shrub/Vine	Berberis thunbergii	Japanese barberry
	Celastrus orbiculatus*	oriental bittersweet
	Euonymus alata	winged burning bush
	Hamamelis virginiana	witch hazel
	Ligustrum vulgare	European privet
	Lindera benzoin	spicebush
	Lonicera japonica*	Japanese honeysuckle
	Lonicera maackii	amur honeysuckle
	Lonicera morrowii	morrow honeysuckle
	Parthenocissus quinquefolia*	Virginia creeper
	Rhodotypos scandens	jetbead
	Rosa multiflora	multiflora rose
	Rubus phoenicolasius	wineberry
	Smilax glauca*	greenbriar
	Toxicodendron radicans*	poison ivy
	Viburnum acerifolium	mapleleaf viburnum
	Viburnum prunifolium	black haw
	Vitis spp.*	grape spp.
	Vitis vulpine*	frost grape
Herb	Alliaria petiolata	garlic mustard
	Allium spp.	wildonion
	Arisaema triphyllum	Jack-in-the-pulpit
	Boehmeria cylindrical	valse nettle
	Cardamine impatiens	bitter-cress
	Carex pensylvanica	Pennsylvania sedge
	Carex spp.	sedge spp.
	Cimicifuga racemosa	black cohosh
	Circaea alpine	enchanger's nightshade
	Claytonia virginica	spring beauty
	Duchesnea indica	Indian strawberry
	Eupatorium purpureum	sweetscented joe pye weed
	Geranium carolianum	wild geranium
	Geum canadense	white avens
	Hepatica nobilis	liverleaf
	Maianthemum racemosum	false solomon's seal
	Microstegium vimineum	Japanese stiltgrass
	Osmorhiza claytoni	sweet cicely
	Oxalis stricta	common yellow wood-sorrel

Vegetation Type Plot	Scientific name	Common name
	Podophyllum peltatum	May apple
	Polygonatum biflorum	smooth solomon's seal
	Polygonum caespitosum	smartweed
	Polygonum virginianum	jumpseed
	Pteridium aquilinum	bracken fern
	Sanguinaria Canadensis	blood root
	Sanicula spp.	snake root
	Symphyotrichum divaricatum	white wood aster
	Uvularia perfoliata	bellwort
	Veronica hederifolia	ivy-leaved speedwell
	Viola spp.	violet spp.
Mount Joy Dry Oak		
Tree	*Acer platanoides*	Norway maple
	Acer rubrum	red maple
	Betula lenta	black birch
	Carya glabra	pignut hickory
	Carya tomentosa	mockernut hickory
	Celtis occidentalis	common hackberry
	Cercis Canadensis	redbud
	Cornus florida	flowering dogwood
	Fagus grandifolia	American beech
	Fraxinus americana	white ash
	Liriodendron tulipifera	tuliptree
	Nyssa sylvatica	blackgum
	Pinus strobus	white pine
	Prunus serotina	black cherry
	Prunus virginiana	choke cherry
	Quercus alba	white oak
	Quercus coccinea	scarlet oak
	Quercus montana	chestnut oak
	Quercus rubra	red oak
	Quercus velutina	black oak
	Sassafras albidum	sassafras
	Ulmus rubra	slippery elm
Shrub/Vine	*Berberis thunbergii*	Japanese barberry
	*Celastrus orbiculatus**	oriental bittersweet
	Euonymus alata	winged burning bush
	Hamamelis virginiana	witch hazel
	Kalmia latifolia	mountain laurel
	Lindera benzoin	spicebush
	*Lonicera japonica**	Japanese honeysuckle
	*Parthenocissus quinquefolia**	Virginia creeper
	Phytolacca americana	pokeweed
	Rhododendron periclymenoides	pink azalea
	Rubus pensilvanicus	Pennsylvania blackberry
	*Smilax glauca**	greenbriar
	*Toxicodendron radicans**	poison ivy
	Vaccinium angustifolium	lowbush blueberry
	Viburnum acerifolium	mapleleaf viburnum
	Viburnum prunifolium	black haw
	*Vitis aestivalis**	summer grape
	Vitis spp.*	grape spp.
Herb	*Alliaria petiolata*	garlic mustard
	Arisaema triphyllum	Jack-in-the-pulpit
	Bartonia virginica	yellow screwstem
	Cardamine impatiens	bitter-cress
	Carrex pensylvanica	Pennsylvania sedge
	Carex spp.	sedge spp.
	Carex swanii	sedge
	Maianthemum racemosum	false solomon's seal
	Microstegium vimineum	Japanese stiltgrass
	Polygonatum biflorum	smooth solomon's seal
	Prenanthes altissima	rattlesnake root
	Thelypteris noveboracensis	New York fern

Vegetation Type Plot	Scientific name	Common name
Mount Misery Dry Oak		
Tree	*Acer platanoides*	Norway maple
	Acer rubrum	red maple
	Betula lenta	black birch
	Carya tomentosa	mockernut hickory
	Castanea dentate	American chestnut
	Cornus florida	flowering dogwood
	Fagus grandifolia	American beech
	Liriodendron tulipifera	tuliptree
	Nyssa sylvatica	blackgum
	Ostrya virginiana	eastern hophornbeam
	Prunus serotina	black cherry
	Quercus alba	white oak
	Quercus coccinea	scarlet oak
	Quercus montana	chestnut oak
	Quercus rubra	red oak
	Quercus velutina	black oak
	Sassafras albidum	sassafras
Shrub/Vine	*Euonymus alata*	winged burning bush
	Gaylussacia baccata	black huckleberry
	Gaylussacia frondosa	blue huckleberry
	Gaylussacia spp.	huckleberry spp.
	Hamamelis virginiana	witch hazel
	Kalmia angustifolia	sheep laurel
	Kalmia latifolia	mountain laurel
	Parthenocissus quinquefolia*	Virginia creeper
	Rhododendron periclymenoides	pink azalea
	Rubus pensilvanicus	Pennsylvania blackberry
	Smilax glauca*	greenbriar
	Toxicodendron radicans*	poison ivy
	Vaccinium angustifolium	lowbush blueberry
	Vaccinium stamineum	deerberry
	Viburnum acerifolium	mapleleaf viburnum
	Viburnum dentatum	arrowwood v burnum
	Viburnum prunifolium	black haw
	Vitis aestivalis*	summer grape
Herb	*Aralia nudicaulis*	wild sarsaparilla
	Carex pensylvanica	Pennsylvania sedge
	Chimaphila maculate	striped pipsissewa
	Dennstaedtia punctilobula	hay scented fern
	Desmodium nudiflorum	naked tick-trefoil
	Gaultheria procumbens	eastern teaberry
	Isotria verticillata	whorled pogonia
	Maianthemum canadense	*wild lily of the valley*
	Maianthemum racemosum	false solomon's seal
	Medeola virginiana	Indian cucumber root
	Microstegium vimineum	Japanese stiltgrass
	Polygonatum biflorum	smooth solomon's seal
	Polygonum caespitosum	smartweed
	Prenanthes altissima	rattlesnake root
	Pteridium aquilinum	bracken fern
	Symphyotrichum divaricatum	white wood aster
	Thelypteris noveboracensis	New York fern
	Uvularia perfoliata	bellwort
	Viola spp.	Violet spp.

* Indicates vining species

NPS 464/119618, January 2013